3.0

WITHDRAWN

REGENTS RESTORATION DRAMA SERIES

General Editor : John Loftis

LOVE FOR LOVE

WILLIAM CONGREVE

Love for Love

Edited by

EMMETT L. AVERY

UNIVERSITY OF NEBRASKA PRESS · LINCOLN

PR
3364
. L7

Regents Restoration Drama Series

The Regents Restoration Drama Series, similar in objectives and format to the Regents Renaissance Drama Series, will provide soundly edited texts, in modern spelling, of the more significant English plays of the late seventeenth and early eighteenth centuries. The word "Restoration" is here used ambiguously and must be explained. If to the historian it refers to the period between 1660 and 1685 (or 1688), it has long been used by the student of drama in default of a more precise word to refer to plays belonging to the dramatic tradition established in the 1660's, weakening after 1700, and displaced in the 1730's. It is in this extended sense—imprecise though justified by academic custom—that the word is used in this series, which will include plays first produced between 1660 and 1737. Although these limiting dates are determined by political events, the return of Charles II (and the removal of prohibitions against the operation of theaters) and the passage of Walpole's Stage Licensing Act, they enclose a period of dramatic history having a coherence of its own in the establishment, development, and disintegration of a tradition.

Each text in the series is based on a fresh collation of the seventeenth- and eighteenth-century editions that might be presumed to have authority. The textual notes, which appear above the rule at the bottom of each page, record all substantive departures from the edition used as the copy-text. Variant substantive readings among contemporary editions are listed there as well. Editions later than the eighteenth century are referred to in the textual notes only when an emendation originating in some one of them is received into the text. Variants of accidentals (spelling, punctuation, capitalization) are not recorded in the notes. Contracted forms of characters' names are silently expanded in speech prefixes and stage directions, and, in the case of speech prefixes, are regularized. Additions to the stage directions of the copy-text are enclosed in brackets. Stage directions such as "within" or "aside" are enclosed in parentheses when they occur in the copy-text.

Spelling has been modernized along consciously conservative lines, but within the limits of a modernized text the linguistic quality of the original has been carefully preserved. Contracted preterites have regularly been expanded. Punctuation has been brought into accord with modern practices. The objective has been to achieve a balance between the pointing of the old editions and a system of punctuation which, without overloading the text with exclamation marks, semi-colons, and dashes, will make the often loosely flowing verse and prose of the original syntactically intelligible to the modern reader. Dashes are regularly used only to indicate interrupted speeches, or shifts of address within a single speech.

Explanatory notes, chiefly concerned with glossing obsolete words and phrases, are printed below the textual notes at the bottom of each page. References to stage directions in the notes follow the admirable system of the Revels editions, whereby stage directions are keyed, decimally, to the line of the text before or after which they occur. Thus, a note on 0.2 has reference to the second line of the stage direction at the beginning of the scene in question. A note on 115.1 has reference to the first line of the stage direction following line 115 of the text of the relevant scene. Speech prefixes, and any stage directions attached to them, are keyed to the first line of accompanying dialogue.

JOHN LOFTIS

Stanford University

Contents

List of Abbreviations

Q1 First edition, *4to.*, Jacob Tonson, 1695

Q2 "Second Edition," *4to.*, Jacob Tonson, 1695

Q3 Another edition, *4to.*, Jacob Tonson, 1695

Q4 "Third Edition," *4to.*, Jacob Tonson, 1697

W1 *The Works*, *8vo.*, Jacob Tonson, 1710

Introduction

The present edition of *Love for Love* is based on the first quarto, Q1, published in 1695. This, the first edition, was followed in the same year by two other quartos, whose priorities are not clear: one, Q2, called "The Second Edition" on the title page, closely based on the first quarto; the other, Q3, a less exact printing, in which the text is crowded into fewer pages. In 1697 appeared another quarto, Q4, called "The Third Edition," which follows the pagination of Q2 but differs in relatively unimportant details. The first collected edition of Congreve's works, W1, published in 1710, has a preface which refers to it as "only recommended as the least faulty Impression." Although this Preface implies that the text has been carefully revised, the only major change from the quartos lies in the systematic division of the acts into scenes. A separate edition dated 1710 is referred to in the Preface of W1 as a "spurious Impression." The present edition lists the textual variants from Q1, omitting those which seem purely accidental misspellings on the part of later compositors.

When *Love for Love* made its first appearance in London on April 30, 1695, William Congreve had a firmly established reputation for comedy. Only two years earlier his first play, *The Old Bachelor*, had appeared in the theater in Drury Lane with an initial run of fourteen consecutive performances, an unusually long run at that time, especially for a first play by an author almost unknown to the literary world. A few months later his second comedy, *The Double Dealer*, was less well received by the public, though generously praised by his friends.

It was a year and a half before he produced his third comedy, *Love for Love*, which ultimately became his most popular drama. It had been ready for the stage at the end of 1694, but controversies within the United Company, which had secured a monopoly of stage productions in 1682, caused him to withhold it until a solution to the conflicts was achieved. During the winter of 1694–1695 a group of dissatisfied actors, led by Thomas Betterton, the foremost player of the period, formed a new company composed of most of the actors who had taken roles in Congreve's two earlier comedies. By the end of March, 1695, the new company had received a license from King William and had secured the old playhouse in Lincoln's Inn Fields for its productions.

Assisted by the good will as well as the generous financial support of the town, Betterton's company rapidly completed the remodeling of the small theater and chose *Love for Love* for its opening attraction. The comedy was a great success. As the anonymous author of *A Comparison Between the Two Stages* (1702) pointed out, it was the "Work of a popular author; but that was not all, the Town was ingag'd in its favour, and in favour of the Actors long before the Play was Acted."[1] Yet if it owed its favorable reception in part to the unusual circumstances of the première, the play was successful in its own right. Like *The Old Bachelor*, it had a fine initial run, this one of thirteen consecutive days. Colley Cibber, then a young actor in the rival company at Drury Lane, stated in his *Apology* (written many years later) that *Love for Love* did so well in the spring of 1695 that the company "had seldom occasion to act any other play" to the end of the season.[2]

The comedy was brilliantly cast. Most of the performers had appeared in Congreve's earlier plays and were expert in comedies of manners. Betterton, who had had leading roles in Congreve's previous comedies, played Valentine; and although he was now within fifteen years of retirement, he still excelled in the sophisticated manner that the role required. Anne Bracegirdle, for whom Congreve created most of his vivacious heroines, acted Angelica. It was Thomas Dogget, however, playing Sailor Ben, who won the greatest acclaim; rumor held that when he was assigned the part, he associated himself with sailors at Wapping to familiarize himself with their language, style, gait, and other mannerisms.[3] Cave Underhill, an experienced comedian who often played "low" or "humours" characters, acted Sir Sampson, and John Bowman, a younger man, played Tattle. Samuel Sandford, a talented actor, took the role of Foresight, the credulous devotee of astrology. Mrs. Foresight and Mrs. Frail, the worldly sisters, were acted by Elizabeth Bowman and Elizabeth Barry. For Miss Prue, the company selected Mrs. Ayliff, who had

---

[1] Ed. S. B. Wells (Princeton: Princeton University Press, 1942), p. 10.

[2] *Apology*, ed. R. W. Lowe (London, 1888), I, 197.

[3] *An Essay on Acting* (London, 1744), p. 10.

successfully played ingenue parts. The Prologue was spoken by Betterton; the Epilogue, by Mrs. Bracegirdle.

The comedy is an exceptionally long one, and the company apparently decided that it had to be shortened. In the Dedication to the printed play Congreve stated that "one whole Scene in the Third Act" was omitted in the presentation. He did not specify the scene but indicated that it was one in which Foresight appeared; and he stressed that it was a passage whose purpose was to develop the design of the plot "with less Precipitation" and to heighten "the ridiculous character of *Foresight*, which indeed seems to be maim'd without it." Recently Anthony Gosse has argued that the scene omitted was that numbered "xi" (Act III) in the collected *Works* published in 1710.[4]

Once established in the repertory, *Love for Love* became Congreve's greatest success in frequency of performance and in regularity of revivals throughout the eighteenth century. Although many critics, in that century and later, held that *The Way of the World* was the dramatist's finest composition, performances of *Love for Love* in the eighteenth century were more frequent and in fact constituted a third of all performances of his plays. During the fifteen years following its première, several members of the original cast—especially Betterton, Mrs. Bracegirdle, Dogget, and Mrs. Barry—continued in their roles. Later, Robert Wilks as Valentine and Anne Oldfield as Angelica contributed to the popularity of the comedy during the first third of the century. Wilks, who was characterized as the "unrivalled *fine gentleman* of the Stage for more than twenty years,"[5] acted Valentine until 1731, while Mrs. Oldfield played Angelica as well as Laetitia (*The Old Bachelor*) and Millamant (*The Way of the World*). Benjamin Johnson, a "humours" actor who delighted in a kinship of name and spirit with Ben Jonson, acted Foresight expertly until 1742, and Colley Cibber frequently played Ben. Barton Booth, one of the triumvirate who governed Drury Lane for many years, sometimes played Scandal, sometimes Valentine. In later years several excellent comedians acted Ben: Josias Miller, John Harper, and Charles

[4] "The Omitted Scene in Congreve's *Love for Love*," *Modern Philology*, LXI (1963), 40–42. Mr. Gosse points out that in the *Works* (1710) Act III is divided into fifteen scenes, of which five (ix–xiii) present Foresight on stage. Scene xi best satisfies Congreve's criterion of a scene which furthers the design and the characterization: in it Scandal encourages Foresight's superstitious nature and prepares the audience for Foresight's comical hypochondria.

[5] Benjamin Victor, *The History of the Theaters* (London, 1761), II, 53.

Macklin; and Hester Santlow (later Mrs. Barton Booth), Mary Bicknell, and Catherine Clive played Prue. In mid-century the Giffards assumed the major roles: Henry as Valentine, William as Scandal, and Mrs. Giffard as Angelica.

Nevertheless, the failure of David Garrick, the supreme actor of the century, to act in *Love for Love* was detrimental to its stage popularity. During Garrick's dominance of the theaters for forty years, *Love for Love* had a fluctuating vogue and rarely was as finely cast as it had been earlier. Its position in the second half of the eighteenth century and in the early nineteenth century was essentially that of a "stock" play, revived occasionally, partly because revivals offered many performers an opportunity to demonstrate their strength and versatility in Congrevean roles. Hence, it was often chosen for benefit performances. Gradually diminishing in vogue in the early nineteenth century, it has been successfully revived in the present century. The Stage Society and the Phoenix Society produced it, as well as Congreve's other comedies, in 1917 at the Aldwych Theater in London, and since that time it has been offered frequently both in London and New York.

The stage success of *Love for Love* in the eighteenth century was due in part, of course, to excellent acting, but its position as the most popular of Congreve's comedies was also due to the simplicity of its plot. Although *The Way of the World* has often been acclaimed as the finest of Congreve's comedies, *Love for Love* has some advantage in its plot, which is easier to follow, both on stage and in print. Essentially it is made up of a series of courtships and intended marriages, one of which comes to a happy consummation, another to a bitter anti-climax. Like most of the situations Congreve contrived, those in *Love for Love* are derived from earlier dramas which were familiar to most spectators—situations turning on interrelated courtships, feigned madness, obsession with astrological portents, and pretension to wit; but the plot is not of such special contrivance that one seeks or finds specific sources for its major complications. Congreve places these actions on various levels of social sophistication and, to give variety to the scenes, introduces several eccentric characters, including, in addition to Foresight, the salty Ben whose natural habitat is the ocean.

To be more specific, the plot centers at its highest level of sophistication in Valentine's pursuit of Angelica, one of Congreve's delightful heroines. Valentine has expended his fortune in casual living and in wooing Angelica, and now faces a financial and romantic crisis. A somewhat reflective man whose libertinism is now partially subdued, he is threatened by his father's decision to settle the whole of his estate on the younger son, Ben, just returned from several years at sea. To avoid signing over his property as a means of paying his debts, Valentine feigns madness. Angelica, financially secure, on the other hand, and seemingly indifferent to Valentine, professes an unwillingness to accept him as a husband. To Valentine her behavior seems to be influenced by perverse whimsy rather than sensible considerations, and he hopes that his pretended madness will cause her to pity and then to love him.

On a much less sophisticated level is the proposed union of Ben the sailor to Miss Prue, a "natural" and impulsive child. Ben, a lively man who speaks plainly (within the confines of his nautical language), considers marriage a state that theoretically he should achieve. He soon finds that Prue loses her natural innocence under the tutelage of Tattle, who teaches her that a woman of society says "No" when she means "Yes" and resists advances although she means to encourage them. He is repelled by her mannerisms, and she considers him a boor compared with Tattle.

To keep these proposed alliances in a further state of cross-purposes, Congreve created Mrs. Frail (her name betrays her character), who pursues Valentine, although she considers marrying Ben if she cannot succeed with Valentine. And he introduced other complications. When Tattle has wearied of Prue, whose prompt compliance bores him, he seeks to win Angelica on the assumption that she has fully rejected Valentine. Finally, Sir Sampson easily persuades himself that marrying Angelica would not only please himself and preserve his fortune but would also punish Valentine. Apart from the main lines of intrigue, Scandal undertakes an affair with Mrs. Foresight.

The complications resolve themselves both happily and ironically. At the last moment, Angelica, moved by Valentine's distress and his magnanimity in resigning his fortune, accepts him. Tattle, gulled into believing that he is marrying Angelica in disguise, and Mrs. Frail, simultaneously thinking that she is marrying the disguised Valentine, find themselves wedded to each other. Irritated with the behavior of both the sophisticated and unsophisticated women, Ben returns to the sea. Angelica candidly tells Valentine that she is "done dissembling now" and is in danger of showing an extreme fondness for him; he promises to dote on her immoderately. Tattle and Mrs. Frail, on the other hand, express hatred for each other.

Some of the characters lack pretense; others are imbued with a falsity of manner. At the beginning, Prue responds naturally to her desires; it is only when she is taught that pretense is the proper mask for a young lady that she turns to the way of the sophisticated world. Ben—direct, natural, and scornful of pretense—cannot adjust to the perversities of society and leaves London. Angelica, generally straightforward in her responses, acknowledges finally as a form of mild dissembling the "coldness which I have always worn before"; and Valentine, who wears an air of worldly ennui and uses the mask of madness, ultimately returns to a simplicity of response and tells Angelica: "If ever you seem to love too much, it must be only when I can't love enough" (V.540–541).[6]

At the other end of the scale, Tattle and Mrs. Frail, utilizing pretense in mood as well as in actual disguises, are defeated by their intrigues and gain each other, the objects they least desire. Sir Sampson, who thought himself a proper father and deluded himself that in middle age he was still young, is reprimanded by Angelica, who wishes to restore him to a proper parental state: "Learn to be a good father, or you'll never get a second wife. I always loved your son, and hated your unforgiving nature. . . . You have not more faults than he has virtues, and 'tis hardly more pleasure to me that I can make him and myself happy, than that I can punish you" (V.504–510). And Foresight, who has believed that the world can be understood and predicted only through the artifices of quadrants, conjunctions, and the proper coordinates of the heavenly spheres, discovers that the actions of the world are not governed by the signs of the zodiac. In general, those who are without pretense win their coveted goals or emerge undamaged; those who live by pretense and do not reform suffer for their folly.

The satire touches upon other subjects. As is characteristic of Congreve's plays, wit is upon every tongue, and the follies of the world are exposed, sometimes lightly, sometimes bitterly. At the opening of the play, for example, when Valentine talks of turning poet, Jeremy, his man, comments: "Ah, pox confound that Will's Coffee-House; it has ruined more young men than the Royal Oak Lottery" (I.80–82). When Valentine suggests that he might use satire, Scandal bluntly asks: "Who would die a martyr to sense in a

6 For an illuminating discussion of some of these alternations between the natural and the pretentious, see Norman N. Holland, *The First Modern Comedies* (Cambridge, Mass., 1959), pp. 161–174.

country where the religion is folly?" (I.128–129). Similarly, the critics, a constant target of all Restoration satirists, receive several thrusts. Scandal once states, "Yes, I have a poet weighing words and selling praise for praise, and a critic picking his pocket. I have another large piece too, representing a school, where there are huge-proportioned critics, with long wigs, laced coats, Steinkirk cravats, and terrible faces, with cat-calls in their hands" (I.575–580).

Valentine's pretense to madness permits Congreve to introduce satire upon a wide range of subjects—not only poetry and criticism, but also the law (which Congreve had once considered as a possible profession), religion, the inconstancy of women, the inconsistency of mankind, the court, and the fashions of the times. Some of these subjects are also satirized in a more straightforward fashion. On one occasion, for example, Valentine and his father wittily comment upon the inconsistency of man's wants. Nearly penniless, Valentine tells his father, "But here I am, and if you don't mean to provide for me, I desire you would leave me as you found me." Sir Sampson accepts the principle: "With all my heart. Come, uncase, strip, and go naked out of the world as you came into't." Valentine's reply is a telling comment: "My clothes are soon put off. But you must also deprive me of reason, thought, passions, inclinations, affections, appetites, senses, and the huge train of attendants that you begot along with me" (II.299–306). And the inconstancy of women is always upon the tongues of the men, though Angelica's demonstration of her affection for Valentine brings from Scandal the admission that although he was once "an infidel to your sex" he is now converted. Yet he considers Angelica a rare exception: "For now I am convinced that all women are not like fortune, blind in bestowing favors, either on those who do not merit, or who do not want 'em" (V.550–553).

Much of the charm of the play, both in reading and in performance, lies in its characterizations and language. Ben's skill with nautical terminology is as beguiling in its way as Sir Sampson's explosive exclamations or Foresight's pedantic discourses upon astrology, the philosophers, the stars and their portents. Ben usually can explain a point only by reference to the sea, and although this aspect of the characterization has an artificial reliance upon a single motif, he is nearly always amusing. "I believe he that marries you will go to sea in a hen-pecked frigate," he says to Mrs. Frail, and adds, "I believe that, young woman, and mayhap may come to an anchor at Cuckold's Point" (IV.380–383). When he is angry with Prue, his rhetoric leaves the nautical for the rhythms of common speech: "But an he [Tattle] comes near me, mayhap I may giv'n a salt eel for's supper, for all that. What does father mean to leave me alone as soon as I come home with such a dirty dowdy? Sea-calf? I an't calf enough to lick your chalked face, you cheese-curd you. Marry thee! Oons, I'll marry a Lapland witch as soon and live upon selling of contrary winds and wrecked vessels" (III.371–377). Ben's style sometimes rubs off on Sir Sampson. Upbraided by Ben for his folly in proposing to marry Angelica, Sir Sampson replies: "Who gave you the authority to speak, sirrah? To your element, fish, be mute, fish, and to sea; rule your helm sirrah, don't direct me" (V.370–372).

In characterizing Foresight and Sir Sampson, Congreve developed other patterns of language. At their best, Foresight's phrases have a lyrical quality that defines him well, as, for example, when he expostulates to Sir Sampson:

> But I tell you, I have traveled, and traveled in the celestial spheres, know the signs and the planets and their houses. Can judge of motions direct and retrograde, of sextiles, quadrates, trines, and oppositions, fiery trigons and aquatical trigons. Know whether life shall be long or short, happy or unhappy, whether diseases are curable or incurable. If journeys shall be prosperous, undertakings successful, or goods stolen recovered, I know.
>
> (II.187–194)

Sir Sampson's apoplectic expressions serve to distinguish him from all the other characters. When Angelica proposes that her lawyer examine the settlement Sir Sampson has outlined, he works himself into a rising crescendo of eloquence:

> With all my heart. Come in with me, and I'll lend you the bond. You shall consult your lawyer, and I'll consult a parson. Odzooks, I'm a young man; odzooks, I'm a young man, and I'll make it appear— Odd, you're devilish handsome; faith and troth, you're very handsome, and I'm very young, and very lusty. Odsbud, hussy, you know how to choose, and so do I. Odd, I think we are very well met. Give me your hand; odd, let me kiss it; 'tis as warm and as soft—as what?—odd, as t'other hand—and give me t'other hand, and I'll mumble 'em, and kiss 'em till they melt in my mouth. (V.123–133)

And few episodes in comedy include such adroit social satire as that in which Mrs. Foresight and Mrs. Frail spar with each other (II.390–431).

Love for Love is, then, a highly readable play which, in the hands of able performers, is a fine stage vehicle. It has variety of characterization within a plot of moderately complex intrigues; the texture of Congreve's language is both compelling and revelatory of the nature and moods of the characters. The satire is penetrating and amusing, if not profound, and the play does more than merely entertain. It presents in broad perspective many facets of human nature. By creating Ben as a "natural" character on an unsophisticated level and by presenting Angelica as a "natural" character in a sophisticated milieu, Congreve brings to comic justice those who deviate foolishly from the standard of good sense and genuine passion.

EMMETT L. AVERY

Washington State University

LOVE FOR LOVE

To the Right Honorable Charles Earl of Dorset and
Middlesex, Lord Chamberlain of His Majesty's Household,
and Knight of the Most Noble Order of the Garter, &c.

MY LORD,

A young poet is liable to the same vanity and indiscretion
with a young lover; and the great man that smiles upon one,
and the fine woman that looks kindly upon t'other are each
of them in danger of having the favor published with the   5
first opportunity.

But there may be a different motive which will a little
distinguish the offenders. For though one should have a
vanity in ruining another's reputation, yet the other may
only have an ambition to advance his own. And I beg leave,   10
my Lord, that I may plead the latter, both as the cause and
excuse of this dedication.

Whoever is king is also the father of his country; and as
nobody can dispute your Lordship's monarchy in poetry,
so all that are concerned ought to acknowledge your   15
universal patronage. And it is only presuming on the
privilege of a loyal subject that I have ventured to make
this, my address of thanks, to your Lordship, which, at the
same time, includes a prayer for your protection.

I am not ignorant of the common form of poetical   20
dedications, which are generally made up of panegyrics,
where the authors endeavor to distinguish their patrons by
the shining characters they give them above other men. But
that, my Lord, is not my business at this time, nor is your
Lordship *now* to be distinguished. I am contented with the 25
honor I do myself in this epistle, without the vanity of
attempting to add to or explain your Lordship's character.

I confess it is not without some struggling that I behave
myself in this case as I ought, for it is very hard to be pleased
with a subject and yet forbear it. But I choose rather to   30
follow Pliny's precept than his example, when in his
panegyric to the Emperor Trajan, he says,

> *Nec minus considerabo quid aures ejus pati possint,*
> *Quam quid virtutibus debeatur.*

33–34. *Nec . . . debeatur*] And I will regard no less what his ears can
tolerate than what is due his virtues.

I hope I may be excused the pedantry of a quotation   35
when it is so justly applied. Here are some lines in the print
(and which your Lordship read before this play was acted)
that were omitted on the stage; and particularly one whole
scene in the third act, which not only helps the design
forward with less precipitation, but also heightens the   40
ridiculous character of Foresight, which indeed seems to be
maimed without it. But I found myself in great danger of a
long play and was glad to help it where I could. Though
notwithstanding my care and the kind reception it had from
the town, I could heartily wish it yet shorter, but the   45
number of different characters represented in it would have
been too much crowded in less room.

This reflection on prolixity (a fault for which scarce any
one beauty will atone) warns me not to be tedious now and
detain your Lordship any longer with the trifles of   50

My Lord,
Your Lordship's Most
Obedient and Most
Humble Servant,
WILL. CONGREVE   55

55. WILL. CONGREVE] *Q1–2, Q4*;
William Congreve *Q3, W1*.

A PROLOGUE
FOR

The opening of the new Playhouse, proposed to
be spoken by Mrs. Bracegirdle in man's clothes.
Sent from an unknown hand.

Custom, which everywhere bears mighty sway,
Brings me to act the orator today;
But women, you will say, are ill at speeches—
'Tis true, and therefore I appear in breeches.
Not for example to you City-wives,   5
That by prescription's settled for your lives.
Was it for gain the husband first consented?
O yes, their gains are mightily augmented.

Making horns with her hands over her head.

And yet, methinks, it must have cost some strife,⎫
A passive husband, and an active wife!   ⎬   10
'Tis awkward, very awkward, by my life.   ⎭
But to my speech—assemblies of all nations⎫
Still are supposed to open with orations; ⎬
Mine shall begin, to show our obligations. ⎭
To you, our benefactors, lowly bowing,   15
Whose favors have prevented our undoing,
A long Egyptian bondage we endured,
Till freedom, by your justice, we procured.
Our taskmasters were grown such very Jews, ⎫
We must at length have played in wooden shoes,⎬   20
Had not your bounty taught us to refuse. ⎭
Freedom's of English growth, I think, alone;
What for lost British freedom can atone?
A free-born player loathes to be compelled;
Our rulers tyrannized, and we rebelled.   25
Freedom! the wise man's wish, the poor man's wealth,
Which you and I and most of us enjoy by stealth,
The soul of pleasure, and the sweet of life,   ⎫
The woman's charter, widow, maid, or wife, ⎬
This they'd have canceled, and thence grew the strife.⎭ 30

17–30.] See Introduction, pp. ix–x.

But you, perhaps, would have me here confess
How we obtained the favor—can't you guess?
Why then, I'll tell you (for I hate a lie),
By brib'ry, arrant brib'ry, let me die.
I was their agent, but by Jove I swear   35
No honorable member had a share,
Though young and able members bid me fair.
I chose a wiser way to make you willing,
Which has not cost the house a single shilling;
Now you suspect at least I went a-billing.   40
You see I'm young, and to that air of youth,
Some will add beauty, and a little truth;
These powerful charms, improved by powerful arts,
Prevailed to captivate your opening hearts.
Thus furnished, I preferred my poor petition,   45
And bribed ye to commiserate our condition.
I laughed, and sighed, and sung, and leered upon ye;
With roguish loving looks, and that way won ye.
The young men kissed me, and the old I kissed,
And luringly I led them as I list.   50
The ladies in mere pity took our parts;
Pity's the darling passion of their hearts.
Thus bribing, or thus bribed, fear no disgraces,
For thus you may take bribes, and keep your places.

PROLOGUE

Spoken at the Opening of the New House,
by Mr. Betterton

The husbandman in vain renews his toil,
To cultivate each year a hungry soil;
And fondly hopes for rich and generous fruit,
When what should feed the tree, devours the root:
Th'unladen boughs, he sees, bode certain dearth,   5
Unless transplanted to more kindly earth.
So, the poor husbands of the stage, who found
Their labors lost upon th'ungrateful ground,
This last and only remedy have proved,
And hope new fruit from ancient stocks removed.   10
Well may they hope, when you so kindly aid,
And plant a soil which you so rich have made.
As Nature gave the world to man's first age,
So from your bounty we receive this stage.
The freedom man was born to, you've restored,⎫   15
And to our world such plenty you afford,   ⎬
It seems like Eden, fruitful of its own accord.⎭
But since in Paradise frail flesh gave way,
And when but two were made, both went astray,
Forbear your wonder and the fault forgive,⎫   20
If in our larger family we grieve   ⎬
One falling Adam and one tempted Eve.⎭
We who remain would gratefully repay   ⎫
What our endeavors can, and bring, this day,⎬
The first-fruit offering of a virgin play.⎭   25
We hope there's something that may please each taste,⎫
And though of homely fare we make the feast,   ⎬
Yet you will find variety at least.⎭
There's humor, which for cheerful friends we got,
And for the thinking party there's a plot.   30
We've something, too, to gratify ill nature
(If there be any here) and that is Satire—
Though Satire scarce dares grin, 'tis grown so mild,

New House] the newly created theater in Lincoln's Inn Fields.

Or only shows its teeth, as if it smiled.
As asses thistles, poets mumble wit,   35
And dare not bite for fear of being bit.
They hold their pens, as swords are held by fools,
And are afraid to use their own edge-tools.
Since the *Plain Dealer*'s scenes of manly rage,
Not one has dared to lash this crying age.   40
This time the poet owns the bold essay,
Yet hopes there's no ill manners in his play.
And he declares by me, he has designed
Affront to none, but frankly speaks his mind.
And should th'ensuing scenes not chance to hit,⎫   45
He offers but this one excuse: 'twas writ ⎬
Before your late encouragement of wit.   ⎭

EPILOGUE

Spoken at the opening of the New House, by Mrs. Bracegirdle

Sure Providence at first designed this place
To be the player's refuge in distress;
For still in every storm they all run hither,
As to a shed that shields 'em from the weather.
But thinking of this change which last befell us, 5
It's like what I have heard our poets tell us:
For when behind our scenes their suits are pleading,
To help their love, sometimes they show their reading,
And wanting ready cash to pay for hearts,
They top their learning on us, and their parts. 10
Once of philosophers they told us stories,
Whom, as I think they called—Py—Pythagories,
I'm sure 'tis some such Latin name they give 'em,
And we, who know no better, must believe 'em.
Now to these men (say they) such souls were given 15
That, after death, ne'er went to hell nor heaven,
But lived, I know not how, in beasts, and then,
When many years were past, in men again.
Methinks, we players resemble such a soul,
That does from bodies, we from houses stroll. 20
Thus Aristotle's soul, of old that was,
May now be damned to animate an ass;
Or in this very house, for aught we know,
Is doing painful penance in some beau;
And this our audience, which did once resort⎫ 25
To shining theaters to see our sport, ⎬
Now find us tossed into a tennis court. ⎭
These walls but t'other day were filled with noise
Of roaring gamesters, and your Damme Boys.
Then bounding balls and racquets they encompassed, 30
And now they're filled with jests and flights and bombast!
I vow I don't much like this transmigration,

---

27. *tennis court*] The theater in Lincoln Inn's Fields had been converted from a tennis court.
29. *Damme Boys*] roistering, swearing men.

Strolling from place to place, by circulation.
Grant heaven we don't return to our first station.
I know not what these think, but for my part   35
I can't reflect, without an aching heart,
How we should end in our original, a cart.
But we can't fear, since you're so good to save us,
That you have only set us up, to leave us.
Thus from the past, we hope for future grace,   40
I beg it—
And some here know I have a begging face.
Then pray continue this your kind behavior,
For a clear stage won't do without your favor.

---

37. *How . . . cart*] Traditionally, Thespis began his acting career by singing ballads in a cart.

44. *clear stage*] one free of debt and control.

DRAMATIS PERSONAE

Men

SIR SAMPSON LEGEND, father to Valentine and Ben	*Mr. Underhill*
VALENTINE, fallen under his father's displeasure by his expensive way of living, in love with Angelica	*Mr. Betterton*
SCANDAL, his friend, a free speaker	*Mr. Smith*
TATTLE, a half-witted beau, vain of his amours, yet valuing himself for secrecy	*Mr. Boman*
BEN, Sir Sampson's younger son, half home-bred and half sea-bred, designed to marry Miss Prue	*Mr. Dogget*
FORESIGHT, an illiterate old fellow, peevish and positive, superstitious, and pretending to understand astrology, palmistry, physiognomy, omens, dreams, etc., uncle to Angelica	*Mr. Sanford*
JEREMY, servant to Valentine	*Mr. Bowen*
TRAPLAND, a scrivener	*Mr. Triffusis*
BUCKRAM, a lawyer	*Mr. Freeman*

Women

ANGELICA, niece to Foresight, of a considerable fortune in her own hands	*Mrs. Bracegirdle*
MRS. FORESIGHT, second wife to Foresight	*Mrs. Bowman*
MRS. FRAIL, sister to Mrs. Foresight, a woman of the town	*Mrs. Barry*
MISS PRUE, daughter to Foresight by a former wife, a silly, awkward country girl	*Mrs. Ayliff*
NURSE, to Miss Prue	*Mrs. Leigh*
JENNY, maid to Angelica	*Mrs. Lawson*

A STEWARD, OFFICERS, SAILORS, AND SEVERAL SERVANTS

The Scene: *In London*

Love for Love

ACT I

Valentine *in his chamber, reading.* Jeremy *waiting. Several books upon the table.*

VALENTINE.

Jeremy.

JEREMY.

Sir.

VALENTINE.

Here, take away. I'll walk a turn and digest what I have read.

JEREMY (*aside, and taking away the books*).

You'll grow devilish fat upon this paper diet.   5

VALENTINE.

And d'ye hear, go you to breakfast. There's a page doubled down in Epictetus that is a feast for an emperor.

JEREMY.

Was Epictetus a real cook or did he only write receipts?

VALENTINE.

Read, read, sirrah, and refine your appetite; learn to live upon instruction; feast your mind, and mortify your flesh;   10 read, and take your nourishment in at your eyes; shut up your mouth, and chew the cud of understanding. So Epictetus advises.

JEREMY.

O Lord! I have heard much of him, when I waited upon a gentleman at Cambridge. Pray, what was that Epictetus?   15

VALENTINE.

A very rich man, not worth a groat.

---

7. *Epictetus*] a Greek Stoic philosopher of the first and second centuries, A.D.

8. *receipts*] recipes.

JEREMY.

Humph, and so he has made a very fine feast, where there
is nothing to be eaten?

VALENTINE.

Yes.

JEREMY.

Sir, you're a gentleman, and probably understand this fine   20
feeding; but if you please, I had rather be at board-wages.
Does your Epictetus, or your Seneca here, or any of these
poor rich rogues, teach you how to pay your debts without
money? Will they shut up the mouths of your creditors?
Will Plato be bail for you? Or Diogenes, because he under-   25
stands confinement, and lived in a tub, go to prison for you?
'Slife, sir, what do you mean, to mew yourself up here with
three or four musty books in commendation of starving and
poverty?

VALENTINE.

Why, sirrah, I have no money, you know it; and therefore   30
resolve to rail at all that have. And in that I but follow the
examples of the wisest and wittiest men in all ages, these
poets and philosophers whom you naturally hate, for just
such another reason: because they abound in sense, and you
are a fool.   35

JEREMY.

Aye, sir, I am a fool. I know it. And yet, Heaven help me,
I'm poor enough to be a wit. But I was always a fool, when
I told you what your expenses would bring you to; your
coaches and your liveries; your treats and your balls; your
being in love with a lady that did not care a farthing for   40
you in your prosperity; and keeping company with wits
that cared for nothing but your prosperity; and now when
you are poor, hate you as much as they do one another.

VALENTINE.

Well, and now I am poor, I have an opportunity to be
revenged on 'em all. I'll pursue Angelica with more love   45
than ever, and appear more notoriously her admirer in this
restraint, than when I openly rivaled the rich fops that made
court to her; so shall my poverty be a mortification to her
pride and, perhaps, make her compassionate that love which

49. that] *Q1-4*; the *W1*.

---

has principally reduced me to this lowness of fortune. And   50
for the wits, I'm sure I'm in a condition to be even with
them.

JEREMY.

Nay, your condition is pretty even with theirs, that's the
truth on't.

VALENTINE.

I'll take some of their trade out of their hands.   55

JEREMY.

Now heaven of mercy continue the tax upon paper; you
don't mean to write!

VALENTINE.

Yes, I do; I'll write a play.

JEREMY.

Hem! Sir, if you please to give me a small certificate of three
lines—only to certify those whom it may concern—that the   60
bearer hereof, Jeremy Fetch by name, has for the space of
seven years truly and faithfully served Valentine Legend,
Esq.; and that he is not now turned away for any mis-
demeanor, but does voluntarily dismiss his master from any
future authority over him—   65

VALENTINE.

No, sirrah, you shall live with me still.

JEREMY.

Sir, it's impossible—I may die with you, starve with you, or
be damned with your works; but to live even three days, the
life of a play, I no more expect it, than to be canonized for
a Muse after my decease.   70

VALENTINE.

You are witty, you rogue! I shall want your help; I'll have
you learn to make couplets, to tag the ends of acts. D'ye
hear, get the maids to Crambo in an evening, and learn the
knack of rhyming. You may arrive at the height of a song
sent by an unknown hand, or a chocolate-house lampoon.   75

JEREMY.

But, sir, is this the way to recover your father's favor? Why,
Sir Sampson will be irreconcilable. If your younger brother
should come from sea, he'd never look upon you again.
You're undone, sir; you're ruined; you won't have a friend

---

73. *Crambo*] a rhyming-verse game.

left in the world if you turn poet. Ah, pox confound that   80
Will's Coffee-House; it has ruined more young men than
the Royal Oak Lottery. Nothing thrives that belongs to't.
The man of the house would have been an alderman by this
time with half the trade, if he had set up in the City. For my
part, I never sit at the door that I don't get double the   85
stomach that I do at a horse race. The air upon Banstead-
Downs is nothing to it for a whetter. Yet I never see it, but
the Spirit of Famine appears to me; sometimes like a
decayed porter, worn out with pimping and carrying *billet-
doux* and songs; not like other porters for hire, but for the   90
jest's sake; now like a thin chairman, melted down to half
his proportion with carrying a poet upon tick to visit some
great fortune; and his fare to be paid him like the wages of
sin, either at the day of marriage, or the day of death.

VALENTINE.

Very well, sir; can you proceed?   95

JEREMY.

Sometimes like a bilked bookseller, with a meager, terrified
countenance, that looks as if he had written for himself, or
were resolved to turn author, and bring the rest of his
brethren into the same condition. And lastly, in the form
of a worn-out punk, with verses in her hand, which her   100
vanity had preferred to settlements, without a whole tatter
to her tail, but as ragged as one of the Muses; or as if she
were carrying her linen to the paper-mill, to be converted
into folio books of warning to all young maids, not to prefer
poetry to good sense, or lying in the arms of a needy wit,   105
before the embraces of a wealthy fool.

Enter Scandal.

SCANDAL.

What, Jeremy holding forth?

106.1.] SCENE II] *W1*.

---

81. *Will's Coffee-House*] in Bow Street, Covent Garden, a popular meeting
place for literati.
82. *Royal Oak Lottery*] one of many popular schemes for raising money.
86–87. *Banstead-Downs*] a popular racing-track in Surrey.
100. *punk*] prostitute.

VALENTINE.

The rogue has (with all the wit he could muster up) been declaiming against wit.

SCANDAL.

Aye? Why then I'm afraid Jeremy has wit, for wherever it 110 is, it's always contriving its own ruin.

JEREMY.

Why, so I have been telling my master, sir. Mr. Scandal, for heaven's sake, sir, try if you can dissuade him from turning poet.

SCANDAL.

Poet! He shall turn soldier first, and rather depend upon the 115 outside of his head than the lining. Why, what the devil, has not your poverty made you enemies enough? Must you needs show your wit to get more?

JEREMY.

Aye, more indeed; for who cares for anybody that has more wit than himself?   120

SCANDAL.

Jeremy speaks like an oracle. Don't you see how worthless great men, and dull rich rogues, avoid a witty man of small fortune? Why, he looks like a writ of enquiry into their titles and estates, and seems commissioned by heaven to seize the better half.   125

VALENTINE.

Therefore I would rail in my writings, and be revenged.

SCANDAL.

Rail? At whom? The whole world? Impotent and vain! Who would die a martyr to sense in a country where the religion is folly? You may stand at bay for awhile; but when the full cry is against you, you won't have fair play for 130 your life. If you can't be fairly run down by the hounds, you will be treacherously shot by the huntsmen. No, turn pimp, flatterer, quack, lawyer, parson, be chaplain to an atheist, or stallion to an old woman—anything but poet. A modern poet is worse, more servile, timorous, and fawning, than 135 any I have named, without you could retrieve the ancient

127. whom?] *Q1*, *Q3–4*, *W1*;
home? *Q2*.

honors of the name, recall the stage of Athens, and be
allowed the force of open honest satire.

VALENTINE.

You are as inveterate against our poets as if your character
had been lately exposed upon the stage. Nay, I am not 140
violently bent upon the trade. (*One knocks.*) Jeremy, see
who's there.   *Exit* Jeremy.
But tell me what you would have me do? What do the
world say of me and my forced confinement?

SCANDAL.

The world behaves itself as it used to do on such occasions: 145
some pity you, and condemn your father; others excuse
him, and blame you; only the ladies are merciful, and wish
you well, since love and pleasurable expense have been
your greatest faults.

Enter Jeremy.

VALENTINE.

How now?   150

JEREMY.

Nothing new, sir. I have dispatched some half a dozen duns
with as much dexterity as a hungry judge does causes at
dinner time.

VALENTINE.

What answer have you given 'em?

SCANDAL.

Patience, I suppose, the old receipt.   155

JEREMY.

No, faith, sir; I have put 'em off so long with patience and
forbearance and other fair words, that I was forced to tell
'em in plain downright English—

VALENTINE.

What?

JEREMY.

That they should be paid.   160

VALENTINE.

When?

JEREMY.

Tomorrow.

VALENTINE.

And how the devil do you mean to keep your word?

JEREMY.

Keep it? Not at all; it has been so very much stretched that
I reckon it will break of course by tomorrow, and nobody   165
be surprised at the matter. (*Knocking.*) Again! Sir, if
you don't like my negotiation, will you be pleased to
answer these yourself.

VALENTINE.

See who they are.   *Exit* Jeremy.
By this, Scandal, you may see what it is to be great!   170
Secretaries of State, Presidents of the Council, and generals
of an army lead just such a life as I do, have just such
crowds of visitants in a morning, all soliciting of past
promises, which are but a civiller sort of duns, that lay
claim to voluntary debts.   175

SCANDAL.

And you, like a true great man, having engaged their
attendance, and promised more than ever you intend to
perform, are more perplexed to find evasions than you would
be to invent the honest means of keeping your word and
gratifying your creditors.   180

VALENTINE.

Scandal, learn to spare your friends, and do not provoke
your enemies; this liberty of your tongue will one day bring
a confinement on your body, my friend.

Re-enter Jeremy.

JEREMY.

O, sir, there's Trapland the scrivener, with two suspicious
fellows like lawful pads, that would knock a man down   185
with pocket-tipstaves. And there's your father's steward,
and the nurse with one of your children from Twitnam.

170.] SCENE III *W1*.   183.1.] SCENE IV *W1*.

---

185. *pads*] bailies (bailiffs) lawfully making arrests by pursuing quarry in
the streets.
186. *pocket-tipstaves*] constables' staves with horned tip.
187. *Twitnam*] Twickenham, Middlesex.

VALENTINE.

Pox on her, could she find no other time to fling my sins
in my face? Here, give her this (*gives money*), and bid her
trouble me no more. [*To* Scandal.] A thoughtless, two- 190
handed whore, she knows my condition well enough, and
might have overlaid the child a fortnight ago, if she had had
any forecast in her.

SCANDAL.

What, is it bouncing Margery and my godson?

JEREMY.

Yes, sir. 195

SCANDAL.

My blessing to the boy, with this token (*gives money*) of my
love. And, d'ee hear, bid Margery put more flocks in her
bed, shift twice a week, and not work so hard, that she may
not smell so vigorously. I shall take the air shortly.

VALENTINE.

Scandal, don't spoil my boy's milk! [*To* Jeremy.] Bid 200
Trapland come in. [*Exit* Jeremy.]
If I can give that Cerberus a sop, I shall be at rest for one
day.

Enter Trapland *and* Jeremy.

O Mr. Trapland! my old friend! Welcome. Jeremy, a chair
quickly, a bottle of sack and a toast—fly—a chair first. 205

TRAPLAND.

A good morning to you, Mr. Valentine, and to you,
Mr. Scandal.

SCANDAL.

The morning's a very good morning, if you don't spoil it.

VALENTINE.

Come sit you down, you know his way.

TRAPLAND (*sits*).

There is a debt, Mr. Valentine, of fifteen hundred pounds 210
of pretty long standing—

194. and] *Q1–4*; with *W1*. 203.1.] SCENE V *W1*.

___

192. *overlaid*] smothered.
197. *flocks*] coarse tufts of wool or cotton for quilting or stuffing.
198. *shift*] change clothing.

VALENTINE.

I cannot talk about business with a thirsty palate. Sirrah,
the sack.

TRAPLAND.

And I desire to know what course you have taken for the
payment.   215

VALENTINE.

Faith and troth, I am heartily glad to see you, my service
to you. Fill, fill, to honest Mr. Trapland. Fuller.

TRAPLAND.

Hold, sweetheart, this is not to our business. My service to
you, Mr. Scandal.   (*Drinks.*)   I have forborne as long—

VALENTINE.

T'other glass, and then we'll talk. Fill, Jeremy.   220

TRAPLAND.

No more, in truth. I have forborne, I say—

VALENTINE [*to* Jeremy].

Sirrah, fill when I bid you. And how does your handsome
daughter? Come, a good husband to her.   *Drinks.*

TRAPLAND.

Thank you. I have been out of this money—

VALENTINE.

Drink first. Scandal, why do you not drink?   *They drink.* 225

TRAPLAND.

And in short, I can be put off no longer.

VALENTINE.

I was much obliged to you for your supply; it did me signal
service in my necessity. But you delight in doing good.
Scandal, drink to me, my friend Trapland's health. An
honester man lives not, nor one more ready to serve his 230
friend in distress, though I say it to his face. Come, fill each
man his glass.

SCANDAL.

What, I know Trapland has been a whoremaster and loves
a wench still. You never knew a whoremaster that was not
an honest fellow.   235

TRAPLAND.

Fie, Mr. Scandal, you never knew—

SCANDAL.

What don't I know? I know the buxom black widow in

the Poultry—eight hundred pounds a year jointure, and
twenty thousand pounds in money. Ahah, old Trap!

VALENTINE.

Say you so, i'faith! Come, we'll remember the widow. 240
I know whereabouts you are. Come, to the widow.

TRAPLAND.

No more, indeed.

VALENTINE.

What, the widow's health. Give it him—off with it.   (*They
drink.*) A lovely girl, i'faith, black, sparkling eyes, soft
pouting ruby lips! Better sealing there than a bond for a 245
million, hah!

TRAPLAND.

No, no, there's no such thing; we'd better mind our
business—you're a wag.

VALENTINE.

No, faith, we'll mind the widow's business. Fill again.
Pretty round heaving breasts, a Barbary shape, and a jut 250
with her bum would stir an anchorite. And the prettiest
foot! O, if a man could but fasten his eyes to her feet, as
they steal in and out, and play at Bo-peep under her
petticoats, ah, Mr. Trapland?

TRAPLAND.

Verily, give me a glass—you're a wag—and here's to the 255
widow.   *Drinks.*

SCANDAL.

He begins to chuckle. Ply him close, or he'll relapse into a
dun.

[*Enter* Snap.]

[SNAP.]

By your leave, gentlemen. Mr. Trapland, if we must do our
office, tell us. We have half a dozen gentlemen to arrest in 260
Pall Mall and Covent Garden; and if we don't make haste
the chairmen will be abroad and block up the chocolate-
houses, and then our labor's lost.

258.1.] SCENE VI *W1.*

---

238. *the Poultry*] a street in London connecting Cheapside and Cornhill.
238. *jointure*] dowry.
250. *a Barbary shape*] Moorish women or steeds, both famous for their
graceful form.

TRAPLAND.

Udso, that's true. Mr. Valentine, I love mirth, but business
must be done. Are you ready to—   265
JEREMY [coming from the door].

Sir, your father's steward says he comes to make proposals
concerning your debts.
VALENTINE.

Bid him come in. Mr. Trapland, send away your officer;
you shall have an answer presently.
TRAPLAND.

Mr. Snap, stay within call.   Exit Snap. 270

Enter Steward and whispers to Valentine.

SCANDAL.

Here's a dog now, a traitor in his wine.   [To Trapland.]
Sirrah, refund the sack. Jeremy, fetch him some warm
water, or I'll rip up his stomach and go the shortest way
to his conscience.
TRAPLAND.

Mr. Scandal, you are uncivil. I did not value your sack, 275
but you cannot expect it again, when I have drunk it.
SCANDAL.

And how do you expect to have your money again, when a
gentleman has spent it?
VALENTINE [to Steward].

You need say no more. I understand the conditions. They
are very hard, but my necessity is very pressing; I agree to 280
'em. Take Mr. Trapland with you, and let him draw the
writing. Mr. Trapland, you know this man; he shall
satisfy you.
TRAPLAND.

Sincerely, I am loath to be thus pressing, but my necessity—
VALENTINE.

No apology, good Mr. Scrivener; you shall be paid.   285
TRAPLAND.

I hope you forgive me, my business requires—
                              Exeunt Steward, Trapland, *and* Jeremy.

270.1.] SCENE VII *WI.*

_____

269. *presently*] immediately.

SCANDAL.

He begs pardon like a hangman at an execution.

VALENTINE.

But I have got a reprieve.

SCANDAL.

I am surprised. What, does your father relent?

VALENTINE.

No, he has sent me the hardest conditions in the world. 290
You have heard of a booby brother of mine, that was sent
to sea three years ago? This brother, my father hears, is
landed; whereupon he very affectionately sends me word,
if I will make a deed of conveyance of my right to his estate
after his death to my younger brother, he will immediately 295
furnish me with four thousand pounds to pay my debts and
make my fortune. This was once proposed before, and I
refused it; but the present impatience of my creditors for
their money, and my own impatience of confinement and
absence from Angelica force me to consent.   300

SCANDAL.

A very desperate demonstration of your love to Angelica.
And I think she has never given you any assurance of hers.

VALENTINE.

You know her temper. She never gave me any great reason
either for hope or despair.

SCANDAL.

Women of her airy temper, as they seldom think before they 305
act, so they rarely give us any light to guess at what they
mean. But you have little reason to believe that a woman of
this age, who has had an indifference for you in your
prosperity, will fall in love with your ill fortune; besides,
Angelica has a great fortune of her own, and great fortunes 310
either expect another great fortune, or a fool.

Enter Jeremy.

JEREMY.

More misfortunes, sir.

VALENTINE.

What, another dun?

287.] SCENE VIII *W1*.   311.1.] SCENE IX *W1*.

JEREMY.

No, sir, but Mr. Tattle is come to wait upon you.

VALENTINE.

Well, I can't help it, you must bring him up; he knows I 315
don't go abroad.   *Exit* Jeremy.

SCANDAL.

Pox on him, I'll be gone.

VALENTINE.

No, prithee stay. Tattle and you should never be asunder;
you are light and shadow, and show one another; he is
perfectly thy reverse both in humor and understanding; and 320
as you set up for defamation, he is a mender of reputations.

SCANDAL.

A mender of reputations! Aye, just as he is a keeper of
secrets, another virtue that he sets up for in the same
manner. For the rogue will speak aloud in the posture of a
whisper, and deny a woman's name, while he gives you the 325
marks of her person. He will forswear receiving a letter from
her, and at the same time show you her hand upon the
superscription. And yet perhaps he has counterfeited the
hand too, and sworn to a truth; but he hopes not to be
believed, and refuses the reputation of a lady's favor, as a 330
doctor says no to a bishopric, only that it may be granted
him. In short, he is a public professor of secrecy, and makes
proclamation that he holds private intelligence. He's here.

Enter Tattle.

TATTLE.

Valentine, good morrow; Scandal, I am yours—that is,
when you speak well of me.   335

SCANDAL.

That is, when I am yours; for while I am my own, or
anybody's else, that will never happen.

TATTLE.

How inhuman!

VALENTINE.

Why, Tattle, you need not be much concerned at anything
that he says, for to converse with Scandal is to play at 340

317.] SCENE X *W1*.   333.1.] SCENE X [*error for XI*] *W1*.

Losing Loadum; you must lose a good name to him, before
you can win it for yourself.

TATTLE.

But how barbarous that is, and how unfortunate for him,
that the world shall think the better of any person for his
calumniation! I thank Heaven, it has always been a part of 345
my character to handle the reputation of others very
tenderly.

SCANDAL.

Ay, such rotten reputations as you have to deal with are to
be handled tenderly indeed.

TATTLE.

Nay, but why rotten? Why should you say rotten, when you 350
know not the persons of whom you speak? How cruel that is!

SCANDAL.

Not know 'em? Why, thou never hadst to do with anybody
that did not stink to all the town.

TATTLE.

Ha, ha, ha! Nay, now you make a jest of it indeed. For there
is nothing more known, than that nobody knows anything 355
of that nature of me. As I hope to be saved, Valentine, I
never exposed a woman since I knew what woman was.

VALENTINE.

And yet you have conversed with several.

TATTLE.

To be free with you, I have—I don't care if I own that. Nay,
more (I'm going to say a bold word now), I never could 360
meddle with a woman that had to do with anybody else.

SCANDAL.

How!

VALENTINE.

Nay, faith, I'm apt to believe him. Except her husband,
Tattle.

TATTLE.

O, that—   365

SCANDAL.

What think you of that noble commoner, Mrs. Drab?

TATTLE.

Pooh, I know Madam Drab has made her brags in three or

---

341. *Losing Loadum*] a card game in which the winner takes no cards.

four places, that I said this and that, and writ to her, and
did I know not what. But, upon my reputation, she did me
wrong. Well, well, that was malice. But I know the bottom 370
of it. She was bribed to that by one that we all know—a man,
too. Only to bring me into disgrace with a certain woman
of quality.

SCANDAL.

Whom we all know.

TATTLE.

No matter for that. Yes, yes, everybody knows—no doubt 375
on't, everybody knows my secrets. But I soon satisfied the
lady of my innocence; for I told her—Madam, says I, there
are some persons who make it their business to tell stories,
and say this and that of one and t'other, and everything in
the world; and, says I, if your grace—   380

SCANDAL.

Grace!

TATTLE.

O Lord, what have I said? My unlucky tongue!

VALENTINE.

Ha, ha, ha!

SCANDAL.

Why, Tattle, thou hast more impudence than one can in
reason expect; I shall have an esteem for thee. Well, and ha, 385
ha, ha! Well, go on, and what did you say to her grace?

VALENTINE.

I confess this is something extraordinary.

TATTLE.

Not a word, as I hope to be saved, an errant *lapsus linguae*.
Come, let's talk of something else.

VALENTINE.

Well, but how did you acquit yourself?   390

TATTLE.

Pooh, pooh, nothing at all, I only rallied with you. A woman
of ordinary rank was a little jealous of me, and I told her
something or other; faith, I know not what. Come, let's
talk of something else.   *Hums a song.*

SCANDAL.

Hang him, let him alone. He has a mind we should inquire. 395

TATTLE.

Valentine, I supped last night with your mistress and

her uncle, old Foresight. I think your father lies at Foresight's.

VALENTINE.

Yes.

TATTLE.

Upon my soul, Angelica's a fine woman. And so is Mrs. 400 Foresight, and her sister, Mrs. Frail.

SCANDAL.

Yes, Mrs. Frail is a very fine woman; we all know her.

TATTLE.

O, that is not fair.

SCANDAL.

What?

TATTLE.

To tell.   405

SCANDAL.

To tell what? Why, what do you know of Mrs. Frail?

TATTLE.

Who, I? Upon honor I don't know whether she be man or woman but by the smoothness of her chin and roundness of her lips.

SCANDAL.

No!   410

TATTLE.

No.

SCANDAL.

She says otherwise.

TATTLE.

Impossible!

SCANDAL.

Yes, faith. Ask Valentine else.

TATTLE.

Why then, as I hope to be saved, I believe a woman only 415 obliges a man to secrecy that she may have the pleasure of telling herself.

SCANDAL.

No doubt on't. Well, but has she done you wrong, or no? You have had her? Ha?

TATTLE.

Though I have more honor than to tell first, I have more 420 manners than to contradict what a lady has declared.

SCANDAL.

Well, you own it?

TATTLE.

I am strangely surprised! Yes, yes, I can't deny it, if she taxes me with it.

SCANDAL.

She'll be here by and by; she sees Valentine every morning. 425

TATTLE.

How!

VALENTINE.

She does me the favor—I mean of a visit sometimes. I did not think that she had granted more to anybody.

SCANDAL.

Nor I, faith. But Tattle does not use to belie a lady; it is contrary to his character. How one may be deceived in a 430 woman, Valentine!

TATTLE.

Nay, what do you mean, gentlemen?

SCANDAL.

I'm resolved I'll ask her.

TATTLE.

O barbarous! Why did you not tell me—

SCANDAL.

No, you told us.   435

TATTLE.

And bid me ask Valentine?

VALENTINE.

What did I say? I hope you won't bring me to confess an answer, when you never asked me the question?

TATTLE.

But, gentlemen, this is the most inhuman proceeding—

VALENTINE.

Nay, if you have known Scandal thus long, and cannot 440 avoid such a palpable decoy as this was, the ladies have a fine time whose reputations are in your keeping.

Enter Jeremy.

JEREMY.

Sir, Mrs. Frail has sent to know if you are stirring.

442.1.] SCENE XI [*error for XII*]
W1.

VALENTINE.

Show her up when she comes.   *Exit* Jeremy.

TATTLE.

I'll be gone.   445

VALENTINE.

You'll meet her.

TATTLE.

Have you not a back way?

VALENTINE.

If there were, you have more discretion than to give Scandal
such an advantage; why, your running away will prove all
that he can tell her.   450

TATTLE.

Scandal, you will not be so ungenerous. O, I shall lose my
reputation of secrecy forever! I shall never be received but
upon public days, and my visits will never be admitted
beyond a drawing room. I shall never see a bedchamber
again, never be locked in a closet, nor run behind a screen, 455
or under a table; never be distinguished among the waiting-
women by the name of trusty Mr. Tattle more. You will
not be so cruel!

VALENTINE.

Scandal, have pity on him. He'll yield to any conditions.

TATTLE.

Any, any terms.   460

SCANDAL.

Come, then, sacrifice half a dozen women of good reputation
to me presently. Come, where are you familiar? And see
that they are women of quality, too, the first quality.

TATTLE.

'Tis very hard. Won't a baronet's lady pass?

SCANDAL.

No, nothing under a right honorable.   465

TATTLE.

O inhuman! You don't expect their names.

SCANDAL.

No, their titles shall serve.

445.] SCENE XII [*error for XIII*] *W1*.

---

465. *right honorable*] a title given to peers and peeresses.

TATTLE.

Alas, that's the same thing. Pray spare me their titles; I'll
describe their persons.

SCANDAL.

Well, begin then. But take notice, if you are so ill a painter 470
that I cannot know the person by your picture of her, you
must be condemned, like other bad painters, to write the
name at the bottom.

TATTLE.

Well, first then—

Enter Mrs. Frail.

O unfortunate! She's come already. Will you have patience 475
'till another time—I'll double the number.

SCANDAL.

Well, on that condition. Take heed you don't fail me.

MRS. FRAIL.

Hey day! I shall get a fine reputation by coming to see
fellows in a morning. Scandal, you devil, are you here too?
O, Mr. Tattle, everything is safe with you, we know.   480

SCANDAL.

Tattle!

TATTLE.

Mum. —O madam, you do me too much honor.

VALENTINE.

Well, Lady Galloper, how does Angelica?

MRS. FRAIL.

Angelica? Manners!

VALENTINE.

What, you will allow an absent lover—   485

MRS. FRAIL.

No, I'll allow a lover present with his mistress to be
particular. But otherwise I think his passion ought to give
place to his manners.

VALENTINE.

But what if he have more passion than manners?

MRS. FRAIL.

Then let him marry and reform.   490

474.1.] SCENE XIII [*error for XIV*] *W1.*

VALENTINE.

Marriage indeed may qualify the fury of his passion, but it
very rarely mends a man's manners.

MRS. FRAIL.

You are the most mistaken in the world; there is no creature
perfectly civil but a husband. For in a little time he grows
only rude to his wife, and that is the highest good breeding,   495
for it begets his civility to other people. Well, I'll tell you
news; but I suppose you hear your brother Benjamin is
landed. And my brother Foresight's daughter is come out
of the country. I assure you, there's a match talked of by the
old people. Well, if he be but as great a sea-beast as she is a   500
land-monster, we shall have a most amphibious breed. The
progeny will be all otters; he has been bred at sea, and she
has never been out of the country.

VALENTINE.

Pox take 'em, their conjunction bodes me no good, I'm sure.

MRS. FRAIL.

Now you talk of conjunction, my brother Foresight has cast   505
both their nativities, and prognosticates an admiral and an
eminent justice of the peace to be the issue-male of their two
bodies. 'Tis the most superstitious old fool! He would have
persuaded me that this was an unlucky day, and would not
let me come abroad. But I invented a dream, and sent him   510
to Artimedorus for interpretation, and so stole out to see you.
Well, and what will you give me now? Come, I must have
something.

VALENTINE.

Step into the next room, and I'll give you something.

SCANDAL.

Aye, we'll all give you something.   515

MRS. FRAIL.

Well, what will you all give me?

VALENTINE.

Mine's a secret.

---

505. *conjunction*] proximity of two heavenly bodies.
511. *Artimedorus*] Artimedorus Daldianus of Ephesus, a second century
(A.D.) interpreter of dreams.

MRS. FRAIL.

I thought you would give me something that would be a
trouble to you to keep.

VALENTINE.

And Scandal shall give you a good name.   520

MRS. FRAIL.

That's more than he has for himself. And what will you give
me, Mr. Tattle?

TATTLE.

I? My soul, madam.

MRS. FRAIL.

Pooh, no, I thank you, I have enough to do to take care of
my own. Well, but I'll come and see you one of these 525
mornings. I hear you have a great many pictures.

TATTLE.

I have a pretty good collection at your service, some
originals.

SCANDAL.

Hang him, he has nothing but the *Seasons* and the *Twelve
Caesars*, paltry copies; and the *Five Senses*, as ill represented 530
as they are in himself; and he himself is the only original
you will see there.

MRS. FRAIL.

Aye, but I hear he has a closet of beauties.

SCANDAL.

Yes, all that have done him favors, if you will believe him.

MRS. FRAIL.

Aye, let me see those, Mr. Tattle.   535

TATTLE.

O, madam, those are sacred to love and contemplation.
No man but the painter and myself was ever blest with the
sight.

MRS. FRAIL.

Well, but a woman—

TATTLE.

Nor woman, 'til she consented to have her picture there 540
too—for then she's obliged to keep the secret.

529–530. *Seasons . . . Twelve Caesars . . . Five Senses*] popular prints of the
day.

SCANDAL.

No, no, come to me if you would see pictures.

MRS. FRAIL.

You?

SCANDAL.

Yes, faith, I can show you your own picture, and most of
your acquaintance to the life, and as like as at Kneller's.   545

MRS. FRAIL.

O lying creature—Valentine, does not he lie?—I can't
believe a word he says.

VALENTINE.

No, indeed, he speaks truth now. For as Tattle has pictures
of all that have granted him favors, he has the pictures of
all that have refused him, if satires, descriptions, characters, 550
and lampoons are pictures.

SCANDAL.

Yes, mine are most in black and white. And yet there are
some set out in their true colors, both men and women.
I can show you pride, folly, affectation, wantonness, inconstancy, covetousness, dissimulation, malice, and ignorance, 555
all in one piece. Then I can show you lying, foppery, vanity,
cowardice, bragging, lechery, impotence, and ugliness in
another piece; and yet one of these is a celebrated beauty,
and t'other a professed beau. I have paintings too, some
pleasant enough.   560

MRS. FRAIL.

Come, let's hear 'em.

SCANDAL.

Why, I have a beau in a bagnio, cupping for a complexion,
and sweating for a shape.

MRS. FRAIL.

So.

SCANDAL.

Then I have a lady burning of brandy in a cellar with a 565
hackney coachman.

---

545. *Kneller's*] Sir Godfrey Kneller, who painted eight "Beauties" for
Queen Mary.
562. *bagnio*] a bathing-house, especially one with hot baths.
562. *cupping*] bleeding, to make a good color.
565. *burning of brandy*] apparently a thrust at Mrs. Frail's reputation.

MRS. FRAIL.

O devil! Well, but that story is not true.

SCANDAL.

I have some hieroglyphics too. I have a lawyer with a hundred hands, two heads, and but one face; a divine with two faces, and one head; and I have a soldier with his brains 570 in his belly, and his heart where his head should be.

MRS. FRAIL.

And no head?

SCANDAL.

No head.

MRS. FRAIL.

Pooh, this is all invention. Have you ne'er a poet?

SCANDAL.

Yes, I have a poet weighing words and selling praise for 575 praise, and a critic picking his pocket. I have another large piece too, representing a school, where there are huge-proportioned critics, with long wigs, laced coats, Steinkirk cravats, and terrible faces, with cat-calls in their hands, and hornbooks about their necks. I have many more of this 580 kind, very well painted, as you shall see.

MRS. FRAIL.

Well, I'll come, if it be only to disprove you.

Enter Jeremy.

JEREMY.

Sir, here's the steward again from your father.

VALENTINE.

I'll come to him. Will you give me leave? I'll wait on you again presently.   585

MRS. FRAIL.

No, I'll be gone. Come, who squires me to the Exchange? I must call my sister Foresight there.

582.1.] SCENE XIV [*error for XV*]
W1.

578–579. *Steinkirk cravats*] a neckcloth popular after the battle of Steenkirke, 1692.

579. *cat-calls*] noisy devices for expressing disapproval of plays.

580. *hornbooks*] leaf of paper containing the alphabet, etc., protected by translucent horn.

SCANDAL.

I will. I have a mind to your sister.

MRS. FRAIL.

Civil!

TATTLE.

I will, because I have a tender for your ladyship.   590

MRS. FRAIL.

That's somewhat the better reason, to my opinion.

SCANDAL.

Well, if Tattle entertains you, I have the better opportunity
to engage your sister.

VALENTINE.

Tell Angelica I am about making hard conditions to come
abroad and be at liberty to see her.   595

SCANDAL.

I'll give an account of you and your proceedings. If indiscretion be a sign of love, you are the most a lover of anybody
that I know: you fancy that parting with your estate will
help you to your mistress. In my mind he is a thoughtless
adventurer,   600

Who hopes to purchase wealth, by selling land;
To win a mistress, with a losing hand.   *Exeunt.*

ACT II

A room in Foresight's House.
Enter Foresight *and* Servant.

FORESIGHT.

Hey day! What, are all the women of my family abroad?
Is not my wife come home? Nor my sister, nor my daughter?

SERVANT.

No, sir.

FORESIGHT.

Mercy on us, what can be the meaning of it? Sure the moon
is in all her fortitudes. Is my niece Angelica at home?   5

SERVANT.

Yes, sir.

FORESIGHT.

I believe you lie, sir.

SERVANT.

Sir?

FORESIGHT.

I say you lie, sir. It is impossible that anything should be as
I would have it; for I was born, sir, when the crab was   10
ascending, and all my affairs go backward.

SERVANT.

I can't tell, indeed, sir.

FORESIGHT.

No, I know you can't, sir. But I can tell, sir, and foretell, sir.

Enter Nurse.

Nurse, where's your young mistress?

NURSE.

Wee'st heart, I know not; they're none of 'em come home   15
yet. Poor child, I warrant she's fond o'seeing the town.
Marry, pray heaven they ha' given her any dinner. Good
lack-a-day, ha ha, ha, O strange! I'll vow and swear now,
ha, ha ha, marry, and did you ever see the like!

13.1.] SCENE II *WI.*

4–5. *moon . . . fortitudes*] the inconstant moon at the height of influence.
10. *crab*] a zodiacal constellation.
15. *Wee'st heart*] contraction of "woe is to the heart."

FORESIGHT.

    Why, how now, what's the matter?   20

NURSE.

    Pray heaven send your worship good luck, marry and amen
with all my heart, for you have put on one stocking with
the wrong side outward.

FORESIGHT.

    Ha, how? Faith and troth, I'm glad of it! and so I have!
That may be good luck in troth, in troth it may, very good   25
luck. Nay, I have had some omens: I got out of bed backwards too this morning, without premeditation; pretty good
that too; but then I stumbled coming down stairs, and met
a weasel; bad omens those. Some bad, some good, our lives
are checkered: mirth and sorrow, want and plenty, night   30
and day, make up our time. But in troth I am pleased at my
stocking; very well pleased at my stocking. O, here's my
niece!

Enter Angelica.

    [*To* Servant.]   Sirrah, go tell Sir Sampson Legend I'll wait
on him if he's at leisure. 'Tis now three o'clock, a very good   35
hour for business; Mercury governs this hour.   *Exit* Servant.

ANGELICA.

    Is it not a good hour for pleasure, too? Uncle, pray lend me
your coach; mine's out of order.

FORESIGHT.

    What, would you be gadding too? Sure all females are mad
today. It is of evil portent, and bodes mischief to the master   40
of a family. I remember an old prophecy written by
Messehalah the Arabian, and thus translated by a reverend
Buckinghamshire bard.

         When housewives all the house forsake,
         And leave good man to brew and bake,   45
         Withouten guile, then be it said,
         That house doth stand upon its head;

37.] SCENE III *WI*.   37. too? Uncle] *Q1, Q3*; too,
                                  uncle? pray *Q2, Q4, WI*.

---

    42. *Messehalah*] a Jewish astrologer of the ninth century.

> And when the head is set in grond,
> Ne marl, if it be fruitful fond.

Fruitful, the head fruitful, that bodes horns; the fruit of the   50
head is horns. Dear niece, stay at home—for by the head of
the house is meant the husband; the prophecy needs no
explanation.

ANGELICA.

Well, but I can neither make you a cuckold, uncle, by
going abroad; nor secure you from being one, by staying at   55
home.

FORESIGHT.

Yes, yes, while there's one woman left, the prophecy is not
in full force.

ANGELICA.

But my inclinations are in force; I have a mind to go abroad;
and if you won't lend me your coach, I'll take a hackney or   60
a chair and leave you to erect a scheme, and find who's in
conjunction with your wife. Why don't you keep her at home
if you're jealous when she's abroad? You know my aunt is
a little retrograde (as you call it) in her nature. Uncle, I'm
afraid you are not lord of the ascendant, ha, ha, ha.   65

FORESIGHT.

Well, Jill-flirt, you are very pert, and always ridiculing that
celestial science.

ANGELICA.

Nay, uncle, don't be angry. If you are, I'll reap up all your
false prophecies, ridiculous dreams, and idle divinations.
I'll swear you are a nuisance to the neighborhood. What a   70
bustle did you keep against the last invisible eclipse, laying
in provision as 'twere for a siege? What a world of fire and
candle, matches and tinderboxes did you purchase! One
would have thought we were ever after to live underground,

---

48. *grond*] an obsolete form of "ground."
49. *Ne marl*] no wonder.
49. *fond*] an obsolete form of "found."
61. *erect a scheme*] make an astrological calculation.
64. *retrograde*] moving in a contrary direction.
65. *lord of the ascendant*] when conditions were such that the astrologer
could make a favorable prediction, the easternmost star in the sign of the
zodiac under which a person was born being lord of the ascendant.

or at least making a voyage to Greenland, to inhabit there   75
all the dark season.

FORESIGHT.

Why, you malapert slut—

ANGELICA.

Will you lend me your coach? or I'll go on—nay, I'll
declare how you prophesied popery was coming, only
because the butler had mislaid some of the apostle's spoons   80
and thought they were lost. Away went religion and spoon-
meat together. Indeed, uncle, I'll indite you for a wizard.

FORESIGHT.

How, hussy! was there ever such a provoking minx?

NURSE.

O merciful father, how she talks!

ANGELICA.

Yes, I can make oath of your unlawful midnight practices;   85
you and the old nurse there—

NURSE.

Marry, heaven defend! I at midnight practices—O Lord,
what's here to do? I in unlawful doings with my master's
worship! Why, did you ever hear the like now? Sir, did
ever I do anything of your midnight concerns—but warm   90
your bed, and tuck you up, and set the candle and your
tobacco-box, and your urinal by you, and now and then
rub the soles of your feet? O Lord, I!

ANGELICA.

Yes, I saw you together, through the keyhole of the closet
one night, like Saul and the Witch of Endor, turning the   95
sieve and shears, and pricking your thumbs, to write poor
innocent servant's names in blood, about a little nutmeg-
grater, which she had forgot in the caudle-cup. Nay, I know
something worse, if I would speak of it—

FORESIGHT.

I defy you, hussy! But I'll remember this, I'll be revenged   100
on you, cockatrice; I'll hamper you. You have your fortune
in your own hands, but I'll find a way to make your lover,

---

80. *apostle's spoons*] spoons bearing the figure of an apostle on the handle,
often given at christenings.
98. *caudle-cup*] a cup of warm drink.

your prodigal spendthrift gallant, Valentine, pay for all, I
will.

ANGELICA.

Will you? I care not, but all shall out then. Look on't, 105
Nurse; I can bring witness that you have a great unnatural
teat under your left arm, and he another; and that you
suckle a young devil in the shape of a tabby-cat, by turns,
I can.

NURSE.

A teat, a teat, I an unnatural teat! O the false, slanderous 110
thing! Feel, feel here, if I have anything but like another
Christian (*crying*) or any teats but two that han't given suck
this thirty years.

FORESIGHT.

I will have patience, since it is the will of the stars I should
be thus tormented. This is the effect of the malicious 115
conjunctions and oppositions in the third house of my
nativity; there the curse of kindred was foretold. But I will
have my doors locked up—I'll punish you, not a man shall
enter my house.

ANGELICA.

Do, uncle, lock 'em up quickly before my aunt comes home. 120
You'll have a letter for alimony tomorrow morning. But let
me be gone first, and then let no mankind come near the
house, but converse with spirits and the celestial signs, the
bull, and the ram, and the goat. Bless me! There are a great
many horned beasts among the twelve signs, uncle. But 125
cuckolds go to heaven.

FORESIGHT.

But there's but one virgin among the twelve signs, spitfire,
but one virgin.

ANGELICA.

Nor there had not been that one, if she had had to do with
anything but astrologers, uncle. That makes my aunt go 130
abroad.

FORESIGHT.

How? How? Is that the reason? Come, you know something; tell me, and I'll forgive you; do, good niece. Come,

---

116. *third house*] one of the twelve parts of the heavens.

you shall have my coach and horses, faith and troth you
shall. Does my wife complain? Come, I know women tell   135
one another. She is young and sanguine, has a wanton hazel
eye, and was born under Gemini, which may incline her to
society; she has a mole upon her lip, with a moist palm, and
an open liberality on the mount of Venus.

ANGELICA.

Ha, ha, ha!   140

FORESIGHT.

Do you laugh? Well, gentlewoman, I'll—but come, be a
good girl, don't perplex your poor uncle, tell me—won't
you speak? Odd, I'll—

Enter Servant.

SERVANT.

Sir Sampson is coming down to wait upon you.

ANGELICA.

Good bye, uncle. [*To* Servant.] Call me a chair.   145
                                        [*Exit* Servant.]
I'll find out my aunt, and tell her she must not come home.
                                          Exit Angelica.

FORESIGHT.

I'm so perplexed and vexed, I am not fit to receive him; I
shall scarce recover myself before the hour be past. Go,
Nurse, tell Sir Sampson I'm ready to wait on him.

NURSE.

Yes, sir.   [*Exit* Nurse.] 150

FORESIGHT.

Well, why if I was born to be a cuckold, there's no more to
be said—

Enter Sir Sampson Legend *with a paper.*

SIR SAMPSON.

Nor no more to be done, old boy; that's plain. Here 'tis,
I have it in my hand, old Ptolemy; I'll make the ungracious

143.1.] SCENE IV *W1*.   already *W1*.
152. said] *Q1–4*; said—he's here   152.1.] SCENE V *W1*.

---

143. *Odd*] a variation of Odso, Godso (God's Son).
154. *old Ptolemy*] Ptolemaeus Alexandrinus, a second-century astrologer.

prodigal know who begat him; I will, old Nostrodamus. 155
What, I warrant my son thought nothing belonged to a
father, but forgiveness and affection; no authority, no
correction, no arbitrary power; nothing to be done, but for
him to offend and me to pardon. I warrant you, if he
danced till doomsday, he thought I was to pay the piper. 160
Well, but here it is under black and white, *signatum*,
sigillatum, and *deliberatum*; that as soon as my son Benjamin
is arrived, he is to make over to him his right of inheritance.
Where's my daughter that is to be? Hah! old Merlin! body
o'me, I'm so glad I'm revenged on this undutiful rogue. 165

FORESIGHT.

Odso, let me see; let me see the paper. Aye, faith and troth,
here 'tis, if it will but hold. I wish things were done and the
conveyance made. When was this signed, what hour? Odso,
you should have consulted me for the time. Well, but we'll
make haste—   170

SIR SAMPSON.

Haste, aye, aye; haste enough. My son Ben will be in town
tonight. I have ordered my lawyer to draw up writings of
settlement and jointure. All shall be done tonight. No matter
for the time; prithee, brother Foresight, leave superstition.
Pox o'th' time; there's no time but the time present, there's 175
no more to be said of what's past, and all that is to come will
happen. If the sun shine by day and the stars by night, why,
we shall know one another's faces without the help of a
candle, and that's all the stars are good for.

FORESIGHT.

How, how? Sir Sampson, that all? Give me leave to 180
contradict you, and tell you, you are ignorant.

SIR SAMPSON.

I tell you I am wise; and *sapiens dominabitur astris*; there's
Latin for you to prove it, and an argument to confound
your Ephemeris. Ignorant! I tell you, I have traveled old

---

155. *old Nostrodamus*] Michel Notre-Dame, sixteenth-century fortune-
teller.

182. *sapiens dominabitur astris*] The wise man will be governed by the
stars.

184. *Ephemeris*] a table of the positions of a heavenly body for any given
period.

Fircu and know the globe. I have seen the Antipodes, where 185
the sun rises at midnight and sets at noonday.

FORESIGHT.

But I tell you, I have traveled, and traveled in the celestial
spheres, know the signs and the planets and their houses.
Can judge of motions direct and retrograde, of sextiles,
quadrates, trines, and oppositions, fiery trigons and 190
aquatical trigons. Know whether life shall be long or short,
happy or unhappy, whether diseases are curable or in-
curable. If journeys shall be prosperous, undertakings
successful, or goods stolen recovered, I know.

SIR SAMPSON.

I know the length of the Emperor of China's foot, have 195
kissed the Great Mogul's slipper, and rid a-hunting upon an
elephant with the Cham of Tartary. Body o'me, I have
made a cuckold of a king, and the present Majesty of Bantam
is the issue of these loins.

FORESIGHT.

I know when travelers lie or speak truth, when they don't 200
know it themselves.

SIR SAMPSON.

I have known an astrologer made a cuckold in the twinkling
of a star, and seen a conjurer that could not keep the devil
out of his wife's circle.

FORESIGHT [aside].

What, does he twit me with my wife too? I must be better 205
informed of this. —Do you mean my wife, Sir Sampson?
Though you made a cuckold of the King of Bantam, yet by
the body of the sun—

SIR SAMPSON.

By the horns of the moon, you would say, Brother Capricorn.

---

185. *Fircu*] an obscure, perhaps fictional, astrologer.
189. *motions . . . retrograde*] movements of the planets, direct and
contrary.
189–191. *sextiles . . . aquatical trigons*] various aspects of the heavenly
bodies.
197. *Cham of Tartary*] reference to traditional Khan of China or Tartary.
198. *Bantam*] a part of Java.
209. *By . . . moon*] satiric play upon cuckolding; see also l. 231.

FORESIGHT.

    Capricorn in your teeth, thou modern Mandevil; Ferdinand 210
Mendez Pinto was but a type of thee, thou liar of the first
magnitude. Take back your paper of inheritance; send your
son to sea again. I'll wed my daughter to an Egyptian
mummy, ere she shall incorporate with a contemner of
sciences and a defamer of virtue.   215

SIR SAMPSON.

    Body o'me, I have gone too far; I must not provoke honest
Albumazar. An Egyptian mummy is an illustrious creature,
my trusty hieroglyphic, and may have significations of
futurity about him; odsbud, I would my son were an
Egyptian mummy for thy sake. What, thou art not angry for 220
a jest, my good Haly? I reverence the sun, moon, and stars
with all my heart. What, I'll make thee a present of a
mummy; now I think on it, body o'me, I have a shoulder
of an Egyptian king that I purloined from one of the
pyramids, powdered with hieroglyphics; thou shalt have it 225
sent home to thy house and make an entertainment for all
the Philomaths and students in physic and astrology in and
about London.

FORESIGHT.

    But what do you know of my wife, Sir Sampson?

SIR SAMPSON.

    Thy wife is a constellation of virtues; she's the moon, and 230
thou art the man in the moon. Nay, she is more illustrious
than the moon, for she has her chastity without her inconstancy. 'S'bud, I was but in jest.

Enter Jeremy.

SIR SAMPSON.

    How now, who sent for you? Ha! what would you have?

233.1.] SCENE VI *W1*.

---

    210. *Mandevil*] reputed author of *The Travels of Sir John Mandeville*.
    211. *Pinto*] a Portuguese adventurer of the sixteenth century.
    217. *Albumazar*] an Arabian astrologer of the ninth century.
    221. *Haly*] an Arabian astronomer of the ninth century.
    227. *Philomaths*] savants; wise men.

FORESIGHT.

Nay, if you were but in jest? Who's that fellow? I don't like 235
his physiognomy.

SIR SAMPSON.

My son, sir. What son, sir? My son Benjamin, hoh?

JEREMY.

No, sir, Mr. Valentine, my master. 'Tis the first time he has
been abroad since his confinement, and he comes to pay his
duty to you.   240

SIR SAMPSON.

Well, sir.

Enter Valentine.

JEREMY.

He is here, sir.

VALENTINE.

Your blessing, sir.

SIR SAMPSON.

You've had it already, sir; I think I sent it you today in a
bill of four thousand pound. A great deal of money, brother 245
Foresight.

FORESIGHT.

Aye, indeed, Sir Sampson, a great deal of money for a
young man; I wonder what he can do with it!

SIR SAMPSON.

Body o'me, so do I. Hark ye, Valentine, if there is too much,
refund the superfluity. Do'st hear, boy?   250

VALENTINE.

Superfluity, sir, it will scarce pay my debts. I hope you will
have more indulgence than to oblige me to those hard
conditions, which my necessity signed to.

SIR SAMPSON.

Sir, how, I beseech you, what were you pleased to intimate
concerning indulgence?   255

VALENTNIE.

Why, sir, that you would not go to the extremity of the
conditions, but release me at least from some part.

SIR SAMPSON.

O, sir, I understand you; that's all, ha?

241.1.] SCENE VII *W1*.

VALENTINE.

Yes, sir, all that I presume to ask. But what you, out of
fatherly kindness, will be pleased to add shall be doubly 260
welcome.

SIR SAMPSON.

No doubt of it, sweet sir, but your filial piety and my
fatherly fondness would fit like two tallies. Here's a rogue,
brother Foresight, makes a bargain under hand and seal in
the morning and would be released from it in the afternoon. 265
Here's a rogue, dog, here's conscience and honesty; this is
your wit now, this is the morality of your wits! You are a
wit, and have been a beau, and may be a—why, sirrah, is
it not here under hand and seal? Can you deny it?

VALENTINE.

Sir, I don't deny it.   270

SIR SAMPSON.

Sirrah, you'll be hanged; I shall live to see you go up
Holborn Hill. Has he not a rogue's face? Speak, brother,
you understand physiognomy; a hanging look to me—of
all my boys the most unlike me. He has a damned Tyburn
face, without the benefit of the clergy.   275

FORESIGHT.

Hum, truly I don't care to discourage a young man; he has
a violent death in his face, but I hope no danger of hanging.

VALENTINE.

Sir, is this usage for your son? For that old weather-headed
fool, I know how to laugh at him; but you, sir—

SIR SAMPSON.

You, sir; and you, sir! Why, who are you, sir?   280

VALENTINE.

Your son, sir.

SIR SAMPSON.

That's more than I know, sir, and I believe not.

VALENTINE.

Faith, I hope not.

---

263. *tallies*] equal or compatible qualities.
272. *Holborn Hill*] on the route from Newgate prison to Tyburn, the site
of executions.

SIR SAMPSON.

What, would you have your mother a whore! Did you
ever hear the like! Did you ever hear the like! Body o'me— 285

VALENTINE.

I would have an excuse for your barbarity and unnatural
usage.

SIR SAMPSON.

Excuse! Impudence! Why, sirrah, mayn't I do what I
please? Are not you my slave? Did not I beget you? And
might not I have chosen whether I would have begot you 290
or no? Ouns, who are you? Whence came you? What
brought you into the world? How come you here, sir?
Here, to stand here, upon those two legs, and look erect
with that audacious face, hah? Answer me that? Did you
come a volunteer into the world? Or did I beat up for you 295
with the lawful authority of a parent, and press you to the
service?

VALENTINE.

I know no more why I came than you do why you called me.
But here I am, and if you don't mean to provide for me, I
desire you would leave me as you found me.   300

SIR SAMPSON.

With all my heart. Come, uncase, strip, and go naked out of
the world as you came into't.

VALENTINE.

My clothes are soon put off. But you must also deprive me
of reason, thought, passions, inclinations, affections,
appetites, senses, and the huge train of attendants that 305
you begot along with me.

SIR SAMPSON.

Body o'me, what a many-headed monster have I
propagated!

VALENTINE.

I am of myself a plain, easy, simple creature, and to be
kept at small expense, but the retinue that you gave me 310
are craving and invincible; they are so many devils that
you have raised and will have employment.

296–297. *volunteer . . . beat up . . . press you*] a play of words upon various
terms of military service.

SIR SAMPSON.

'Oons, what had I to do to get children? Can't a private
man be born without all these followers? Why, nothing
under an emperor should be born with appetites. Why, at 315
this rate a fellow that has but a groat in his pocket may
have a stomach capable of a ten-shilling ordinary.

JEREMY.

Nay, that's as clear as the sun. I'll make oath of it before
any justice in Middlesex.

SIR SAMPSON.

Here's a cormorant, too. 'S'heart, this fellow was not born 320
with you? I did not beget him, did I?

JEREMY.

By the provision that's made for me, you might have begot
me too. Nay, and to tell your worship another truth, I
believe you did, for I find I was born with those same
whoreson appetites, too, that my master speaks of.   325

SIR SAMPSON.

Why, look you there, now. I'll maintain it, that by the rule
of right reason, this fellow ought to have been born without
a palate. 'S'heart, what should he do with a distinguishing
taste? I warrant now he'd rather eat a pheasant than a
piece of poor John; and smell, now, why I warrant he can 330
smell, and loves perfumes above a stink. Why, there's it, and
music—don't you love music, scoundrel?

JEREMY.

Yes, I have a reasonable good ear, sir, as to jigs and country
dances, and the like; I don't much matter your solos or
sonatas; they give me the spleen.   335

SIR SAMPSON.

The spleen, ha, ha, ha, a pox confound you. Solos and
sonatas? 'Oons, whose son are you? How were you
engendered, muckworm?

JEREMY.

I am by my father, the son of a chairman; my mother sold

---

317. *ten-shilling ordinary*] a dining place with a ten-shilling (expensive)
meal.

320. *cormorant*] a large bird, figuratively a greedy person.

330. *poor John*] a piece of dried fish.

oysters in winter and cucumbers in summer; and I came 340
upstairs into the world, for I was born in a cellar.

FORESIGHT.

By your looks, you should go upstairs out of the world too,
friend.

SIR SAMPSON.

And if this rogue were anatomized now, and dissected, he
has his vessels of digestion and concoction, and so forth, 345
large enough for the inside of a cardinal, this son of a
cucumber. These things are unaccountable and unreasonable. Body o'me, why was not I a bear, that my cubs might
have lived upon sucking their paws? Nature has been
provident only to bears and spiders; the one has its nutri- 350
ment in his own hands, and t'other spins his habitation out
of his entrails.

VALENTINE.

Fortune was provident enough to supply all the necessities
of my nature, if I had my right of inheritance.

SIR SAMPSON.

Again! 'Oons, han't you four thousand pound?—if I had 355
it again, I would not give thee a groat. What, wouldst thou
have me turn pelican and feed thee out of my own vitals?
'S'heart, live by your wits. You were always fond of the
wits; now let's see if you have wit enough to keep yourself.
Your brother will be in town tonight, or tomorrow morning, 360
and then look you perform covenants, and so your friend
and servant. Come, brother Foresight.

> *Exeunt* Sir Sampson *and* Foresight.

JEREMY.

I told you what your visit would come to.

VALENTINE.

'Tis as much as I expected. I did not come to see him;
I came to Angelica, but since she was gone abroad, it was 365
easily turned another way, and at least looked well on my
side. What's here? Mrs. Foresight and Mrs. Frail; they are
earnest. I'll avoid 'em. Come this way, and go and inquire
when Angelica will return.   [*Exeunt* Valentine *and* Jeremy.]

363.] SCENE VIII *W1.*

---

345. *concoction*] one of the various stages of the digestive process.
368. *earnest*] in close or serious conversation.

Enter Mrs. Foresight *and* Mrs. Frail.

MRS. FRAIL.

What have you to do to watch me? 'Slife, I'll do what I 370
please.

MRS. FORESIGHT.

You will?

MRS. FRAIL.

Yes, marry will I. A great piece of business to go to Covent
Garden Square in a hackney-coach and take a turn with
one's friend.   375

MRS. FORESIGHT.

Nay, two or three turns, I'll take my oath.

MRS. FRAIL.

Well, what if I took twenty?—I warrant if you had been
there, it had been only innocent recreation. Lord, where's
the comfort of this life if we can't have the happiness of
conversing where we like?   380

MRS. FORESIGHT.

But can't you converse at home? I own it, I think there's no
happiness like conversing with an agreeable man; I don't
quarrel at that, nor I don't think but your conversation was
very innocent; but the place is public, and to be seen with
a man in a hackney-coach is scandalous. What if anybody 385
else should have seen you alight, as I did? How can anybody
be happy, while they're in perpetual fear of being seen
and censured? Besides, it would not only reflect upon you,
sister, but me.

MRS. FRAIL.

Pooh, here's a clutter. Why should it reflect upon you? I 390
don't doubt but you have thought yourself happy in a
hackney-coach before now. If I had gone to Knightsbridge,
or to Chelsea, or to Spring-Garden, or Barn-Elms with a
man alone—something might have been said.

MRS. FORESIGHT.

Why, was I ever in any of these places? What do you mean, 395
sister?

369.1.] SCENE IX *W1.*

---

373. *marry*] exclamation conveying "yes" or "surely."

392–393. *Knightsbridge . . . Barn-Elms*] fashionable resorts, some with
unenviable reputations.

MRS. FRAIL.

Was I? What do you mean?

MRS. FORESIGHT.

You have been at a worse place.

MRS. FRAIL.

I at a worse place, and with a man!

MRS. FORESIGHT.

I suppose you would not go alone to the World's-End?   400

MRS. FRAIL.

The World's-End! What, do you mean to banter me?

MRS. FORESIGHT.

Poor innocent! You don't know that there's a place called
the World's-End? I'll swear you can keep your countenance
purely; you'd make an admirable player.

MRS. FRAIL.

I'll swear you have a great deal of impudence, and in my 405
mind too much for the stage.

MRS. FORESIGHT.

Very well, that will appear who has most. You never were
at the World's-End?

MRS. FRAIL.

No.

MRS. FORESIGHT.

You deny it positively to my face.   410

MRS. FRAIL.

Your face, what's your face?

MRS. FORESIGHT.

No matter for that; it's as good a face as yours.

MRS. FRAIL.

Not by a dozen years' wearing. But I do deny it positively to
your face then.

MRS. FORESIGHT.

I'll allow you now to find fault with my face; for I'll swear 415
your impudence has put me out of countenance. But look
you here now—where did you get this gold bodkin?—O,
sister, sister!

---

400. *World's End*] another resort.
417. *bodkin*] a pin or pin-shaped ornament.

MRS. FRAIL.

My bodkin!

MRS. FORESIGHT.

Nay, 'tis yours, look at it.   420

MRS. FRAIL.

Well, if you go to that, where did you find this bodkin?
O, sister, sister! Sister every way.

MRS. FORESIGHT [*aside*].

O devil on't, that I could not discover her without betraying
myself.

MRS. FRAIL.

I have heard gentlemen say, sister, that one should take 425
great care, when one makes a thrust in fencing, not to lie
open one's self.

MRS. FORESIGHT.

It's very true, sister. Well, since all's out, and as you say,
since we are both wounded, let us do that is often done in
duels, take care of one another, and grow better friends 430
than before.

MRS. FRAIL.

With all my heart. Ours are but slight flesh wounds, and if
we keep 'em from air, not at all dangerous. Well, give me
your hand in token of sisterly secrecy and affection.

MRS. FORESIGHT.

Here 'tis with all my heart.   435

MRS. FRAIL.

Well, as an earnest of friendship and confidence, I'll
acquaint you with a design that I have. To tell truth and
speak openly one to another: I'm afraid the world have
observed us more than we have observed one another.
You have a rich husband and are provided for; I am at a 440
loss and have no great stock either of fortune or reputation,
and therefore must look sharply about me. Sir Sampson has
a son that is expected tonight, and by the account I have
heard of his education, can be no conjurer. The estate, you
know, is to be made over to him. Now if I could wheedle 445
him, sister, ha? You understand me?

423. *discover*] disclose, bring into fuller knowledge.
444. *conjurer*] one who is not clever.

MRS. FORESIGHT.

I do, and will help you to the utmost of my power. And I
can tell you one thing that falls out luckily enough: my
awkward daughter-in-law, who, you know, is designed for
his wife, is grown fond of Mr. Tattle. Now if we can improve 450
that and make her have an aversion for the booby, it may
go a great way towards his liking of you. Here they come
together; and let us contrive some way or other to leave
'em together.

Enter Tattle *and* Miss Prue.

MISS PRUE.

Mother, mother, mother, look you here.   455

MRS. FORESIGHT.

Fie, fie, Miss, how you bawl. Besides, I have told you, you
must not call me mother.

MISS PRUE.

What must I call you then? Are not you my father's wife?

MRS. FORESIGHT.

Madam; you must say madam. By my soul, I shall fancy
myself old indeed, to have this great girl call me mother. 460
Well, but, Miss, what are you so overjoyed at?

MISS PRUE.

Look you here, madam then, what Mr. Tattle has given
me. Look you here, cousin, here's a snuff-box; nay, there's
snuff in't. Here, will you have any? O good! How sweet it is.
Mr. Tattle is all over sweet, his peruke is sweet, and his 465
gloves are sweet, and his handkerchief is sweet, pure sweet,
sweeter than roses. Smell him, mother, madam, I mean.
He gave me this ring for a kiss.

TATTLE.

O fie, Miss, you must not kiss and tell.

MISS PRUE.

Yes, I may tell my mother. And he says he'll give me 470
something to make me smell so. O, pray lend me your
handkerchief. Smell, cousin; he says he'll give me something

454.1.] SCENE X *W1*.

---

449. *daughter-in-law*] stepdaughter.
465. *peruke*] skull-cap covered with hair, like a wig.

that will make my smocks smell this way. Is not it pure?
It's better than lavender, mun. I'm resolved I won't let
nurse put any more lavender among my smocks, ha, cousin? 475

MRS. FRAIL.

Fie, Miss; amongst your linen, you must say. You must
never say smock.

MISS PRUE.

Why, it is not bawdy, is it, cousin?

TATTLE.

O, madam, you are too severe upon Miss; you must not
find fault with her pretty simplicity, it becomes her 480
strangely. Pretty Miss, don't let 'em persuade you out of
your innocency.

MRS. FORESIGHT.

O, demn you, toad! I wish you don't persuade her out of
her innocency.

TATTLE.

Who, I, madam? O Lord, how can your ladyship have such 485
a thought? Sure, you don't know me?

MRS. FRAIL.

Ah, devil, sly devil. He's as close, sister, as a confessor. He
thinks we don't observe him.

MRS. FORESIGHT.

A cunning cur, how soon he could find out a fresh harmless
creature; and left us, sister, presently.   490

TATTLE.

Upon reputation—

MRS. FORESIGHT.

They're all so, sister, these men—they love to have the
spoiling of a young thing; they are as fond of it, as of being
first in the fashion, or of seeing a new play the first day. I
warrant it would break Mr. Tattle's heart to think that 495
anybody else should be beforehand with him.

TATTLE.

O Lord, I swear I would not for the world—

MRS. FRAIL.

O hang you! who'll believe you? You'd be hanged before

---

473. *pure*] fine, excellent, capital.
474. *mun*] man.

you'd confess. We know you—she's very pretty!—Lord,
what pure red and white!—she looks so wholesome; ne'er 500
stir, I don't know, but I fancy, if I were a man—

MISS PRUE.

How you love to jeer one, cousin.

MRS. FORESIGHT.

Hark'ee, sister, by my soul the girl is spoiled already. D'ee
think she'll ever endure a great lubberly tarpaulin? Gad, I
warrant you, she won't let him come near her, after Mr. 505
Tattle.

MRS. FRAIL.

O'my soul, I'm afraid not—eh!—filthy creature, that smells
all of pitch and tar! Devil take you, you confounded toad—
why did you see her before she was married?

MRS. FORESIGHT.

Nay, why did we let him? My husband will hang us. He'll 510
think we brought 'em acquainted.

MRS. FRAIL.

Come, faith, let us be gone. If my brother Foresight should
find us with them, he'd think so, sure enough.

MRS. FORESIGHT.

So he would. But then, leaving 'em together is as bad. And
he's such a sly devil, he'll never miss an opportunity.   515

MRS. FRAIL.

I don't care; I won't be seen in't.

MRS. FORESIGHT.

Well, if you should, Mr. Tattle, you'll have a world to
answer for. Remember I wash my hands of it; I'm thoroughly
innocent.   *Exeunt* Mrs. Foresight *and* Mrs. Frail.

MISS PRUE.

What makes 'em go away, Mr. Tattle? What do they 520
mean—do you know?

TATTLE.

Yes, my dear, I think I can guess. But hang me if I know the
reason of it.

MISS PRUE.

Come, must not we go too?

TATTLE.

No, no, they don't mean that.   525

520.] SCENE XI *W1.*

MISS PRUE.

No! What then? What shall you and I do together?

TATTLE.

I must make love to you, pretty Miss. Will you let me make
love to you?

MISS PRUE.

Yes, if you please.

TATTLE [aside].

Frank, I gad, at least. What a pox does Mrs. Foresight 530
mean by this civility? Is it to make a fool of me? Or does
she leave us together out of good morality. and do as she
would be done by? Gad, I'll understand it so.

MISS PRUE.

Well, and how will you make love to me? Come, I long to
have you begin. Must I make love too? You must tell me 535
how.

TATTLE.

You must let me speak, Miss; you must not speak first. I
must ask you questions, and you must answer.

MISS PRUE.

What, is it like the catechism? Come, then, ask me.

TATTLE.

D'ye think you can love me?   540

MISS PRUE.

Yes.

TATTLE.

Pooh, pox, you must not say yes already; I shan't care a
farthing for you then in a twinkling.

MISS PRUE.

What must I say then?

TATTLE.

Why, you must say no, or you believe not, or you can't tell. 545

MISS PRUE.

Why, must I tell a lie then?

TATTLE.

Yes, if you would be well-bred. All well-bred persons lie.
Besides, you are a woman; you must never speak what you
think. Your words must contradict your thoughts, but your
actions may contradict your words. So, when I ask you if 550
you can love me, you must say no, but you must love me
too. If I tell you you are handsome, you must deny it and

say I flatter you, but you must think yourself more charming than I speak you. And like me, for the beauty which I say you have, as much as if I had it myself. If 555 I ask you to kiss me, you must be angry, but you must not refuse me. If I ask you for more, you must be more angry, but more complying; and as soon as ever I make you say you'll cry out, you must be sure to hold your tongue.   560

MISS PRUE.

O Lord, I swear this is pure. I like it better than our old-fashioned country way of speaking one's mind. And must not you lie too?

TATTLE.

Hum—yes—but you must believe I speak truth.

MISS PRUE.

O Gemini! Well, I always had a great mind to tell lies, but 565 they frighted me and said it was a sin.

TATTLE.

Well, my pretty creature, will you make me happy by giving me a kiss?

MISS PRUE.

No, indeed; I'm angry at you.   *Runs and kisses him.*

TATTLE.

Hold, hold, that's pretty well, but you should not have given 570 it me, but have suffered me to take it.

MISS PRUE.

Well, we'll do it again.

TATTLE.

With all my heart. Now, then, my little angel.   *Kisses her.*

MISS PRUE.

Pish.

TATTLE.

That's right. Again, my charmer.   *Kisses again.* 575

MISS PRUE.

O fie, nay, now I can't abide you.

TATTLE.

Admirable! That was as well as if you had been born and bred in Covent Garden all the days of your life. And won't you show me, pretty Miss, where your bedchamber is?   580

MISS PRUE.

    No, indeed, won't I, but I'll run there and hide myself from
you behind the curtains.

TATTLE.

    I'll follow you.

MISS PRUE.

    Ah, but I'll hold the door with both hands and be angry,
and you shall push me down before you come in.   585

TATTLE.

    No, I'll come in first, and push you down afterwards.

MISS PRUE.

    Will you? Then I'll be more angry, and more complying.

TATTLE.

    Then I'll make you cry out.

MISS PRUE.

    O, but you shan't, for I'll hold my tongue.

TATTLE.

    O, my dear apt scholar.   590

MISS PRUE.

    Well, now, I'll run and make more haste than you.

Exit Miss Prue.

TATTLE.

    You shall not fly so fast as I'll pursue.   *Exit after her.*

      The End of the Second Act

ACT III

Enter Nurse.

NURSE.

Miss, Miss, Miss Prue. Mercy on me, marry and amen.
Why, what's become of the child? Why, Miss, Miss
Foresight! Sure she has not locked herself up in her chamber,
and gone to sleep, or to prayers. Miss, Miss! I hear her.
Come to your father, child. Open the door. Open the door,   5
Miss. I hear you cry husht. O Lord, who's there? (*Peeps.*)
What's here to do? O the Father! A man with her! Why,
Miss, I say, God's my life, here's fine doings towards—O
Lord, we're all undone. O you young harlotry. (*Knocks.*)
Od's my life, won't you open the door? I'll come in the   10
back way.   *Exit.*

Tattle *and* Miss [Prue] *at the door.*

MISS PRUE.

O Lord, she's coming, and she'll tell my father. What shall
I do now?

TATTLE.

Pox take her. If she had stayed two minutes longer, I should
have wished for her coming.   15

MISS PRUE.

O dear, what shall I say? Tell me, Mr. Tattle, tell me a lie.

TATTLE.

There's no occasion for a lie; I could never tell a lie to no
purpose. But since we have done nothing, we must say
nothing, I think. I hear her. I'll leave you together, and
come off as you can.   *Thrusts her in, and shuts the door.*   20

Enter Valentine, Scandal, *and* Angelica.

ANGELICA.

You can't accuse me of inconstancy; I never told you that
I loved you.

VALENTINE.

But I can accuse you of uncertainty, for not telling me
whether you did or no.

11.1.] SCENE II *W1.*   20.1.] SCENE III *W1.*

ANGELICA.

You mistake indifference for uncertainty; I never had   25
concern enough to ask myself the question.

SCANDAL.

Nor good nature enough to answer him that did ask you.
I'll say that for you, madam.

ANGELICA.

What, are you setting up for good nature?

SCANDAL.

Only for the affectation of it, as the women do for ill nature.   30

ANGELICA.

Persuade your friend that it is all affectation.

VALENTINE.

I shall receive no benefit from the opinion, for I know no
effectual difference between continued affectation and
reality.

TATTLE (*coming up. Aside to* Scandal).

Scandal, are you in private discourse, anything of secrecy?   35

SCANDAL.

Yes, but I dare trust you. We were talking of Angelica's love
for Valentine; you won't speak of it.

TATTLE.

No, no, not a syllable. I know that's a secret, for it's
whispered everywhere.

SCANDAL.

Ha, ha, ha.   40

ANGELICA.

What is, Mr. Tattle? I heard you say something was
whispered everywhere.

SCANDAL.

Your love of Valentine.

ANGELICA.

How!

TATTLE.

No, madam, his love for your ladyship. Gad take me, I beg   45
your pardon, for I never heard a word of your ladyship's
passion till this instant.

ANGELICA.

My passion! And who told you of my passion, pray, sir?

SCANDAL.

Why, is the devil in you? Did not I tell it you for a secret?

TATTLE.

Gadso, but I thought she might have been trusted with her   50
own affairs.

SCANDAL.

Is that your discretion? Trust a woman with herself?

TATTLE.

You say true, I beg your pardon. I'll bring it off— It was
impossible, madam, for me to imagine that a person of
your ladyship's wit and gallantry could have so long   55
received the passionate address of the accomplished
Valentine, and yet remain insensible; therefore, you will
pardon me if from a just weight of his merit, with your
ladyship's good judgment, I formed the balance of a
reciprocal affection.   60

VALENTINE.

O the devil, what damned costive poet has given thee this
lesson of fustian to get by rote?

ANGELICA.

I dare swear you wrong him; it is his own. And Mr. Tattle
only judges of the success of others from the effects of his
own merit. For certainly Mr. Tattle was never denied   65
anything in his life.

TATTLE.

O Lord! yes indeed, madam, several times.

ANGELICA.

I swear I don't think 'tis possible.

TATTLE.

Yes, I vow and swear I have. Lord, madam, I'm the most
unfortunate man in the world, and the most cruelly used by   70
the ladies.

ANGELICA.

Nay, now you're ungrateful.

TATTLE.

No, I hope not. 'Tis as much ingratitude to own some favors
as to conceal others.

---

61. *costive*] close, confined, or (satirically) constipated.
62. *fustian*] figuratively: inflated, turgid, coarse.

VALENTINE.

There, now it's out. 75

ANGELICA.

I don't understand you now. I thought you had never asked anything but what a lady might modestly grant, and you confess.

SCANDAL.

So faith, your business is done here; now you may go brag somewhere else. 80

TATTLE.

Brag! O Heavens! Why, did I name anybody?

ANGELICA.

No, I suppose it is not in your power, but you would if you could, no doubt on't.

TATTLE.

Not in my power, madam! What, does your ladyship mean that I have no woman's reputation in my power? 85

SCANDAL (aside).

Ouns, why you won't own it, will you?

TATTLE.

Faith, madam, you're in the right. No more I have, as I hope to be saved; I never had it in my power to say anything to a lady's prejudice in my life. For as I was telling you, madam, I have been the most unsuccessful creature living in 90 things of that nature, and never had the good fortune to be trusted once with a lady's secret, not once.

ANGELICA.

No.

VALENTINE.

Not once, I dare answer for him.

SCANDAL.

And I'll answer for him, for I'm sure if he had, he would 95 have told me. I find, madam, you don't know Mr. Tattle.

TATTLE.

No indeed, madam, you don't know me at all, I find, for sure my intimate friends would have known—

ANGELICA.

Then it seems you would have told, if you had been trusted.

TATTLE.

O pox, Scandal, that was too far put. Never have told 100

particulars, madam. Perhaps I might have talked as of a third person, or have introduced an amour of my own in conversation by way of novel; but never have explained particulars.

ANGELICA.

But whence comes the reputation of Mr. Tattle's secrecy if 105 he was never trusted?

SCANDAL.

Why thence it arises—the thing is proverbially spoken, but may be applied to him—as if we should say in general terms, he only is secret who never was trusted: a satirical proverb upon our sex. There's another upon yours: as she is chaste 110 who was never asked the question. That's all.

VALENTINE.

A couple of very civil proverbs, truly. 'Tis hard to tell whether the lady or Mr. Tattle be the more obliged to you, for you found her virtue upon the backwardness of the men, and his secrecy upon the mistrust of the women.   115

TATTLE.

Gad, it's very true, madam, I think we are obliged to acquit ourselves. And for my part—but your ladyship is to speak first—

ANGELICA.

Am I? Well, I freely confess I have resisted a great deal of temptation.   120

TATTLE.

And I, gad, I have given some temptation that has not been resisted.

VALENTINE.

Good.

ANGELICA.

I cite Valentine here, to declare to the court how fruitless he has found his endeavors, and to confess all his solicita- 125 tions and my denials.

VALENTINE.

I am ready to plead not guilty for you, and guilty for myself.

SCANDAL.

So, why this is fair, here's demonstration with a witness.

TATTLE.

Well, my witnesses are not present. But I confess I have had 130

favors from persons, but as the favors are numberless, so
the persons are nameless.

SCANDAL.

Pooh, pox, this proves nothing.

TATTLE.

No? I can show letters, lockets, pictures, and rings, and if
there be occasion for witnesses, I can summon the maids at 135
the chocolate-houses, all the porters of Pall Mall and Covent
Garden, the doorkeepers at the playhouse, the drawers at
Locket's, Pontack's, the Rummer, Spring-Garden; my own
landlady and *valet de chambre*; all who shall make oath that I
receive more letters than the secretary's office, and that I 140
have more vizor-masks to inquire for me than ever went to
see the hermaphrodite or the naked prince. And it is
notorious that in a country church, once, an inquiry being
made who I was, it was answered, I was the famous Tattle,
who had ruined so many women.   145

VALENTINE.

It was there, I suppose, you got the nickname of the Great
Turk.

TATTLE.

True, I was called Turk-Tattle all over the parish. The next
Sunday all the old women kept their daughters at home, and
the parson had not half his congregation. He would have 150
brought me into the spiritual court, but I was revenged upon
him, for he had a handsome daughter, whom I initiated into
the science. But I repented it afterwards, for it was talked of
in town. And a lady of quality that shall be nameless, in a
raging fit of jealousy, came down in her coach and six 155
horses, and exposed herself upon my account. Gad, I was
sorry for it with all my heart. You know whom I mean; you
know where we raffled—

SCANDAL.

Mum, Tattle.

VALENTINE.

'Sdeath, are not you ashamed?   160

---

138. *Locket's ... Spring-Garden*] fashionable eating places.
142. *hermaphrodite ... prince*] two of several popular shows in London.
158. *where we raffled*] Sometimes ladies' reputations were raffled off,
a sum of money being divided into equal parts and shares disposed of by
casting lots.

ANGELICA.

O barbarous! I never heard so insolent a piece of vanity.
Fie, Mr. Tattle, I'll swear I could not have believed it.
Is this your secrecy?

TATTLE.

Gadso, the heat of my story carried me beyond my discretion,
as the heat of the lady's passion hurried her beyond her 165
reputation. But I hope you don't know whom I mean, for
there were a great many ladies raffled. Pox on't, now could
I bite off my tongue.

SCANDAL.

No, don't, for then you'll tell us no more. Come, I'll recom-
mend a song to you upon the hint of my two proverbs, and 170
I see one in the next room that will sing it.   *Goes to the door.*

TATTLE.

For heaven's sake, if you do guess, say nothing. Gad, I'm
very unfortunate.

Re-enter Scandal, *with one to sing.*

SCANDAL.

Pray sing the first song in the last new play.

SONG
Set by Mr. John Eccles

A nymph and a swain to Apollo once prayed;   175
The swain had been jilted, the nymph been betrayed.
Their intent was to try if his oracle knew
E'er a nymph that was chaste, or a swain that was true.

Apollo was mute, and had like t'have been posed,
But sagely at length he this secret disclosed: 180
He alone won't betray in whom none will confide,
And the nymph may be chaste that has never been tried.

Enter Sir Sampson, Mrs. Frail, Miss [Prue], *and* Servant.

---

169. No, don't] *Q4, W1*; No doubt   174.2.] SCENE IV *W1.*
on't, *Q1–3.*

174.2. *John Eccles*] a leading composer, who supplied music for many
plays.
179. *posed*] grave or composed.

SIR SAMPSON.

Is Ben come? Odso, my son Ben come? Odd, I'm glad on't.
Where is he? I long to see him. Now, Mrs. Frail, you shall
see my son Ben. Body o'me, he's the hopes of my family. 185
I han't seen him these three years; I warrant he's grown.
Call him in; bid him make haste. I'm ready to cry for joy.

Exit Servant.

MRS. FRAIL.

Now, Miss, you shall see your husband.

MISS PRUE (*aside to* Mrs. Frail.)

Pish, he shall be none of my husband.

MRS. FRAIL.

Hush. Well, he shan't. Leave that to me. —I'll beckon 190
Mr. Tattle to us.

ANGELICA.

Won't you stay and see your brother?

VALENTINE.

We are the twin stars and cannot shine in one sphere. When
he rises I must set. Besides, if I should stay, I don't know
but my father in good nature may press one to the immediate 195
signing the deed of conveyance of my estate, and I'll defer
it as long as I can. Well, you'll come to a resolution.

ANGELICA.

I can't. Resolution must come to me, or I shall never have
one.

SCANDAL.

Come, Valentine, I'll go with you; I've something in my 200
head to communicate to you.   *Exit* Valentine *and* Scandal.

SIR SAMPSON.

What, is my son Valentine gone? What, is he sneaked off
and would not see his brother? There's an unnatural
whelp! There's an ill-natured dog! What, were you here too,
madam, and could not keep him! Could neither love, nor 205
duty, nor natural affection oblige him? Odsbud, madam,
have no more to say to him; he is not worth your consideration. The rogue has not a dram of generous love
about him—all interest, all interest; he's an undone

202.] SCENE V *W1.*

---

193. *twin stars*] figuratively, of equal power, therefore incompatible.

scoundrel, and courts your estate. Body o'me, he does not 210
care a doit for your person.

ANGELICA.

I'm pretty even with him, Sir Sampson, for if ever I could
have liked anything in him, it should have been his estate
too. But since that's gone, the bait's off, and the naked hook
appears.   215

SIR SAMPSON.

Odsbud, well spoken, and you are a wiser woman than I
thought you were; for most young women nowadays are to
be tempted with a naked hook.

ANGELICA.

If I marry, Sir Sampson, I'm for a good estate with any
man, and for any man with a good estate; therefore, if I 220
were obliged to make a choice, I declare I'd rather have
you than your son.

SIR SAMPSON.

Faith and troth, you're a wise woman, and I'm glad to
hear you say so; I was afraid you were in love with the
reprobate. Odd, I was sorry for you with all my heart. 225
Hang him, mongrel! Cast him off; you shall see the rogue
show himself and make love to some desponding Cadua of
fourscore for sustenance. Odd, I love to see a young spendthrift forced to cling to an old woman for support, like ivy
round a dead oak. Faith, I do; I love to see 'em hug and 230
cotton together, like down upon a thistle.

Enter Ben[jamin] Legend *and* Servant.

BEN.

Where's father?

SERVANT.

There, sir, his back's toward you.

SIR SAMPSON.

My son Ben! Bless thee, my dear boy; body o'me, thou art
heartily welcome.   235

231.1.] SCENE VI *W1.*

---

227. *Cadua*] an obscure word probably referring to an elderly woman
seeking admiration or courtship.
  231. *cotton*] agree, fraternize.

BEN.

Thank you, father, and I'm glad to see you.

SIR SAMPSON.

Odsbud, and I'm glad to see thee. Kiss me, boy; kiss me again and again, dear Ben.   *Kisses him.*

BEN.

So, so, enough, father; mess, I'd rather kiss these gentle-women.   240

SIR SAMPSON.

And so thou shalt. Mrs. Angelica, my son Ben.

BEN.

Forsooth an you please. (*Salutes her.*) Nay, mistress, I'm not for dropping anchor here. About ship, i'faith. (*Kisses* Mrs. Frail.) Nay, and you too, my little cockboat—so. (*Kisses* Miss Prue.)

TATTLE.

Sir, you're welcome ashore.   245

BEN.

Thank you, thank you, friend.

SIR SAMPSON.

Thou hast been many a weary league, Ben, since I saw thee.

BEN.

Ay, ay, been! Been far enough, an that be all. Well, father, and how do all at home? How does brother Dick, and brother Val?   250

SIR SAMPSON.

Dick, body o'me, Dick has been dead these two years; I writ you word when you were at Leghorn.

BEN.

Mess, and that's true; marry, I had forgot. Dick's dead, as you say—well, and how? I have a many questions to ask you. Well, you ben't married again, father, be you?   255

SIR SAMPSON.

No, I intend you shall marry, Ben; I would not marry for thy sake.

BEN.

Nay, what does that signify? An you marry again—why,

---

239. *mess*] by the mass.
248. *an*] if.

then, I'll go to sea again, so there's one for t'other, an that
be all. Pray don't let me be your hindrance; e'en marry, a 260
God's name, an the wind sit that way. As for my part,
mayhap I have no mind to marry.

MRS. FRAIL.

That would be pity, such a handsome young gentleman.

BEN.

Handsome! he, he, he, nay, forsooth, an you be for joking,
I'll joke with you, for I love my jest, an the ship were 265
sinking, as we sayn at sea. But I'll tell you why I don't much
stand towards matrimony. I love to roam about from port
to port and from land to land; I could never abide to be
port-bound, as we call it. Now a man that is married has,
as it were, d'ee see, his feet in the bilboes, and mayhap 270
mayn't get 'em out again when he would.

SIR SAMPSON.

Ben's a wag.

BEN.

A man that is married, d'ee see, is no more like another man
than a galley slave is like one of us free sailors; he is chained
to an oar all his life, and mayhap forced to tug a leaky 275
vessel into the bargain.

SIR SAMPSON.

A very wag, Ben's a very wag; only a little rough, he wants
a little polishing.

MRS. FRAIL.

Not at all. I like his humor mightily; it's plain and honest.
I should like such a humor in a husband extremely.   280

BEN.

Say'n you so, forsooth? Marry, and I should like such a
handsome gentlewoman for a bedfellow hugely. How say
you, mistress, would you like going to sea? Mess, you're a
tight vessel and well rigged, and you were but as well
manned.   285

MRS. FRAIL.

I should not doubt that if you were master of me.

BEN.

But I'll tell you one thing, an you come to sea in a high wind,

---

270. *bilboes*] shackles for confining prisoners.

or that lady [*pointing to* Angelica], you mayn't carry so much
sail o'your head—top and top-gallant, by the mess.

MRS. FRAIL.

No, why so?   290

BEN.

Why an you do, you may run the risk to be overset, and
then you'll carry your keels above water, he, he he.

ANGELICA.

I swear, Mr. Benjamin is the veriest wag in nature, an
absolute sea-wit.

SIR SAMPSON.

Nay, Ben has parts, but as I told you before, they want a 295
little polishing. You must not take anything ill, madam.

BEN.

No, I hope the gentlewoman is not angry. I mean all in good
part. For if I give a jest, I'll take a jest, and so forsooth you
may be as free with me.

ANGELICA.

I thank you, sir, I am not at all offended, but methinks, 300
Sir Sampson, you should leave him alone with his mistress.
Mr. Tattle, we must not hinder lovers.

TATTLE [*aside to* Miss Prue].

Well, Miss, I have your promise.

SIR SAMPSON.

Body o'me, madam, you say true. Look you, Ben, this is
your mistress. Come, Miss, you must not be shamefaced; 305
we'll leave you together.

MISS PRUE.

I can't abide to be left alone. Mayn't my cousin stay with
me?

SIR SAMPSON.

No, no, come let's away.

BEN.

Look you, father, mayhap the young woman mayn't take a 310
liking to me.

SIR SAMPSON.

I warrant thee, boy. Come, come, we'll be gone; I'll venture
that.   *Exeunt all but* Ben *and* Miss Prue.

---

289. *top and top-gallant*] top sail and top-gallant sail, i.e., with all sails set.

BEN.

> Come, mistress, will you please to sit down? For an you
> stand astern a that'n, we shall never grapple together. 315
> Come, I'll haul a chair; there, an you please to sit, I'll sit
> by you.

MISS PRUE.

> You need not sit so near one; if you have anything to say,
> I can hear you farther off; I an't deaf.

BEN.

> Why, that's true, as you say, nor I an't dumb; I can be 320
> heard as far as another. I'll heave off to please you. (*Sits
> farther off.*) An we were a league asunder, I'd undertake
> to hold discourse with you, an 'twere not a main high wind
> indeed, and full in my teeth. Look you forsooth, I am, as it
> were, bound for the land of matrimony; 'tis a voyage, d'ee 325
> see, that was none of my seeking. I was commanded by
> father, and if you like of it, mayhap I may steer into your
> harbor. How say you, mistress? The short of the thing is this,
> that if you like me, and I like you, we may chance to swing
> in a hammock together.   330

MISS PRUE.

> I don't know what to say to you, nor I don't care to speak
> with you at all.

BEN.

> No, I'm sorry for that. But pray, why are you so scornful?

MISS PRUE.

> As long as one must not speak one's mind, one had better not
> speak at all, I think, and truly I won't tell a lie for the 335
> matter.

BEN.

> Nay, you say true in that; it's but a folly to lie, for to speak
> one thing and to think just the contrary way is, as it were,
> to look one way and to row another. Now, for my part, d'ee
> see, I'm for carrying things above board; I'm not for 340
> keeping anything under hatches, so that if you ben't as
> willing as I, say so, a God's name; there's no harm done.
> Mayhap you may be shamefaced; some maidens, tho'f they

314.] SCENE VII *W1*.

---

315. *astern a that'n*] if you stand back to me.

love a man well enough, yet they don't care to tell'n so to's
face. If that's the case, why silence gives consent.   345

MISS PRUE.

But I'm sure it is not so, for I'll speak sooner than you
should believe that; and I'll speak truth, tho' one should
always tell a lie to a man; and I don't care, let my father do
what he will! I'm too big to be whipped, so I'll tell you
plainly. I don't like you, nor love you at all, nor never will, 350
that's more; so there's your answer for you, and don't
trouble me no more, you ugly thing.

BEN.

Look you, young woman, you may learn to give good
words, however; I spoke you fair, d'ee see, and civil. As for
your love or your liking, I don't value it of a rope's end, 355
and mayhap I like you as little as you do me. What I said
was in obedience to Father; gad, I fear a whipping no more
than you do. But I tell you one thing, if you should give
such language at sea, you'd have a cat-o'-nine-tails laid
cross your shoulders. Flesh! who are you? You heard t'other 360
handsome young woman speak civilly to me of her own
accord. Whatever you think of yourself, gad, I don't think
you are any more to compare to her than a can of small
beer to a bowl of punch.

MISS PRUE.

Well, and there's a handsome gentleman, and a fine 365
gentleman, and a sweet gentleman, that was here that
loves me, and I love him; and if he sees you speak to me
any more, he'll thrash your jacket for you, you great sea-
calf.

BEN.

What, do you mean that fair-weather spark that was here 370
just now? Will he thrash my jacket? Let'n—let'n. But an he
comes near me, mayhap I may giv'n a salt eel for's supper,
for all that. What does father mean to leave me alone as
soon as I come home with such a dirty dowdy? Sea-calf?
I an't calf enough to lick your chalked face, you cheese-curd 375
you. Marry thee! Oons, I'll marry a Lapland witch as soon
and live upon selling of contrary winds and wrecked vessels.

---

372. *giv'n a salt eel*] possibly, to throw him overboard.

MISS PRUE.

I won't be called names, nor I won't be abused thus, so I won't. If I were a man—(cries)—you durst not talk at this rate. No, you durst not, you stinking tar-barrel.   380

Enter Mrs. Foresight *and* Mrs. Frail.

MRS. FORESIGHT.

They have quarreled just as we could wish.

BEN.

Tar-barrel? Let your sweetheart there call me so, if he'll take your part, your Tom Essence, and I'll say something to him. Gad, I'll lace his musk-doublet for him; I'll make him stink; he shall smell more like a weasel than a civet cat, 385 afore I ha' done with 'en.

MRS. FORESIGHT.

Bless me, what's the matter, Miss? What, does she cry? Mr. Benjamin, what have you done to her?

BEN.

Let her cry. The more she cries, the less she'll— She has been gathering foul weather in her mouth, and now it 390 rains out at her eyes.

MRS. FORESIGHT.

Come, Miss, come along with me, and tell me, poor child.

MRS. FRAIL.

Lord, what shall we do? There's my brother Foresight and Sir Sampson coming. Sister, do you take Miss down into the parlor, and I'll carry Mr. Benjamin into my chamber, 395 for they must not know that they are fallen out. Come, sir, will you venture yourself with me?   *Looks kindly on him.*

BEN.

Venture, mess, and that I will, though 'twere to sea in a storm.   *Exeunt.*

Enter Sir Sampson *and* Foresight.

SIR SAMPSON.

I left 'em together here. What, are they gone? Ben's a brisk 400 boy. He has got her into a corner, father's own son; faith,

380.1.] SCENE VIII *W1*.   *W1*; matter? Miss, what *Q1*.
387. matter, Miss? What] *Q2–4*,   399.1.] SCENE IX *W1*.

384. *musk-doublet*] dark brown apparel, possibly perfumed.

he'll tousle her, and mousle her. The rogue's sharp set,
coming from sea; if he should not stay for saying grace, old
Foresight, but fall to without the help of a parson, ha?
Odd, if he should I could not be angry with him; 'twould 405
be but like me, a chip of the old block. Ha! thou'rt
melancholy, old prognostication, as melancholy as if thou
hadst spilt the salt or pared thy nails of a Sunday. Come,
cheer up, look about thee. Look up, old stargazer. Now is he
poring upon the ground for a crooked pin or an old horse- 410
nail, with the head towards him.

FORESIGHT.

Sir Sampson, we'll have the wedding tomorrow morning.

SIR SAMPSON.

With all my heart.

FORESIGHT.

At ten o'clock, punctually at ten.

SIR SAMPSON.

To a minute, to a second; thou shall set thy watch, and the 415
bridegroom shall observe its motions; they shall be married
to a minute, go to bed to a minute, and when the alarm
strikes, they shall keep time like the figures of St. Dunstan's
clock, and *consummatum est* shall ring all over the parish.

Enter Scandal.

SCANDAL.

Sir Sampson, sad news.   420

FORESIGHT.

Bless us!

SIR SAMPSON.

Why, what's the matter?

SCANDAL.

Can't you guess at what ought to afflict you and him, and
all of us, more than anything else?

SIR SAMPSON.

Body o'me, I don't know any universal grievance, but a new 425
tax and the loss of the Canary Fleet. Without Popery should

419.1.] SCENE X *W1*.

---

402. *tousle and mousle*] dishevel and pull about roughly.
426. *Canary Fleet*] in the summer of 1694 Lord Russell searched the seas
without success to engage the French ships.

be landed in the west, or the French fleet were at anchor in
Blackwall.

SCANDAL.

No. Undoubtedly Mr. Foresight knew all this, and might
have prevented it.   430

FORESIGHT.

'Tis no earthquake!

SCANDAL.

No, not yet, nor whirlwind. But we don't know what it may
come to—but it has had a consequence already that
touches us all.

SIR SAMPSON.

Why, body o'me, out with't.   435

SCANDAL.

Something has appeared to your son Valentine. He's gone
to bed upon't, and very ill. He speaks little, yet says he has
a world to say. Asks for his father and the wise Foresight,
talks of Raymond Lully, and the ghost of Lilly. He has
secrets to impart, I suppose, to you two. I can get nothing   440
out of him but sighs. He desires he may see you in the
morning, but would not be disturbed tonight, because he
has some business to do in a dream.

SIR SAMPSON.

Hoity toity! What have I to do with his dreams or his
divination? Body o'me, this is a trick to defer signing the   445
conveyance. I warrant the devil will tell him in a dream
that he must not part with his estate. But I'll bring him a
parson to tell him that the devil's a liar. Or if that won't do,
I'll bring a lawyer that shall out-lie the devil. And so I'll
cry whether my blackguard or his shall get the better of the 450
day.   *Exit.*

SCANDAL.

Alas, Mr. Foresight, I'm afraid all is not right. You are a
wise man, and a conscientious man, a searcher into
obscurity and futurity, and if you commit an error, it is
with a great deal of consideration, and discretion, and   455
caution—

452.] SCENE XI *W1.*

---

439. *Raymond Lully*] a philosopher-theologian of the thirteenth century.
439. *Lilly*] William Lilly, a contemporary astrologer.

FORESIGHT.

Ah, good Mr. Scandal—

SCANDAL.

Nay, nay, 'tis manifest; I do not flatter you. But Sir Sampson
is hasty, very hasty; I'm afraid he is not scrupulous enough,
Mr. Foresight. He has been wicked, and Heaven grant he 460
may mean well in his affair with you, but my mind gives
me, these things cannot be wholly insignificant. You are
wise, and should not be overreached; methinks you should
not—

FORESIGHT.

Alas, Mr. Scandal, *humanum est errare*.   465

SCANDAL.

You say true, man will err, mere man will err, but you are
something more. There have been wise men, but they were
such as you, men who consulted the stars and were observers
of omens. Solomon was wise, but how?—by his judgment
in astrology. So says Pineda in his third book and eighth 470
chapter.

FORESIGHT.

You are learned, Mr. Scandal!

SCANDAL.

A trifler, but a lover of art; and the wise men of the East
owed their instruction to a star, which is rightly observed
by Gregory the Great in favor of astrology! And Albertus 475
Magnus makes it the most valuable science, because, says
he, it teaches us to consider the causation of causes, in the
causes of things.

FORESIGHT.

I protest I honor you, Mr. Scandal; I did not think you had
been read in these matters. Few young men are inclined— 480

SCANDAL.

I thank my stars that have inclined me. But I fear this
marriage and making over this estate, this transferring of a
rightful inheritance, will bring judgments upon us. I
prophesy it, and I would not have the fate of Cassandra,
not to be believed. Valentine is disturbed; what can be the 485
cause of that? And Sir Sampson is hurried on by an unusual

---

470. *Pineda*] Juan de Pineda, a theologian of the sixteenth century.
475–476. *Albertus Magnus*] the great thirteenth-century theologian.

violence. I fear he does not act wholly from himself;
methinks he does not look as he used to do.

FORESIGHT.

He was always of an impetuous nature. But as to this
marriage I have consulted the science, and all appearances 490
are prosperous.

SCANDAL.

Come, come, Mr. Foresight, let not the prospect of worldly
lucre carry you beyond your judgment, nor against your
conscience. You are not satisfied that you act justly.

FORESIGHT.

How! 495

SCANDAL.

You are not satisfied, I say. I am loath to discourage you,
but it is palpable that you are not satisfied.

FORESIGHT.

How does it appear, Mr. Scandal? I think I am very well
satisfied.

SCANDAL.

Either you suffer yourself to deceive yourself, or you do not 500
know yourself.

FORESIGHT.

Pray explain yourself.

SCANDAL.

Do you sleep well o'nights?

FORESIGHT.

Very well.

SCANDAL.

Are you certain? You do not look so. 505

FORESIGHT.

I am in health, I think.

SCANDAL.

So was Valentine this morning, and looked just so.

FORESIGHT.

How! Am I altered any way! I don't perceive it.

SCANDAL.

That may be, but your beard is longer than it was two hours
ago. 510

490. science] *Q1–3*; stars *Q4, W1.*

FORESIGHT.

Indeed! Bless me.

Enter Mrs. Foresight.

MRS. FORESIGHT.

Husband, will you go to bed? It's ten o'clock. Mr. Scandal, your servant.

SCANDAL.

Pox on her, she has interrupted my design, but I must work her into the project. You keep early hours, madam.   515

MRS. FORESIGHT.

Mr. Foresight is punctual; we sit up after him.

FORESIGHT.

My dear, pray lend me your glass, your little looking glass.

SCANDAL.

Pray lend it him, madam; I'll tell you the reason.

(*She gives him the glass;* Scandal *and she whisper.*)

My passion for you is grown so violent that I am no longer master of myself. I was interrupted in the morning, when 520 you had charity enough to give me your attention, and I had hopes of finding another opportunity of explaining myself to you, but was disappointed all this day, and the uneasiness that has attended me ever since brings me now hither at this unseasonable hour.   525

MRS. FORESIGHT.

Was there ever such impudence, to make love to me before my husband's face? I'll swear I'll tell him.

SCANDAL.

Do, I'll die a martyr, rather than disclaim my passion. But come a little farther this way, and I'll tell you what project I had to get him out of the way, that I might have an 530 opportunity of waiting upon you.   *Whisper.*

FORESIGHT (*looking in the glass*).

I do not see any revolution here. Methinks I look with a serene and benign aspect—pale, a little pale—but the roses of these cheeks have been gathered many years. Ha! I do not like that sudden flushing—gone already!—hem, hem, 535 hem! faintish. My heart is pretty good, yet it beats; and my

511.1.] SCENE XII *W1*.

pulses, ha!—I have none—mercy on me—hum. Yes, here
they are. Gallop, gallop, gallop, gallop, gallop, gallop, hey!
Whither will they hurry me? Now they're gone again. And
now I'm faint again, and pale again, and hem! and my hem! 540
—breath, hem!—grows short; hem! hem! he, he, hem!

SCANDAL.

It takes; pursue it in the name of love and pleasure.

MRS. FORESIGHT.

How do you do, Mr. Foresight?

FORESIGHT.

Hum, not so well as I thought I was. Lend me your hand.

SCANDAL.

Look you there now. Your lady says your sleep has been 545
unquiet of late.

FORESIGHT.

Very likely.

MRS. FORESIGHT.

O mighty restless, but I was afraid to tell him so. He has
been subject to talking and starting.

SCANDAL.

And did not use to be so.   550

MRS. FORESIGHT.

Never, never, 'til within these three nights. I cannot say that
he has once broken my rest since we have been married.

FORESIGHT.

I will go to bed.

SCANDAL.

Do so, Mr. Foresight, and say your prayers. He looks better
than he did.   555

MRS. FORESIGHT.

Nurse, Nurse!

FORESIGHT.

Do you think so, Mr. Scandal?

SCANDAL.

Yes, yes, I hope this will be gone by morning, taking it in
time.

FORESIGHT.

I hope so.   560

Enter Nurse.

560.1.] SCENE XIII *W1.*

MRS. FORESIGHT.

Nurse, your master is not well. Put him to bed.

SCANDAL.

I hope you will be able to see Valentine in the morning.
You had best take a little diacodian and cowslip water, and
lie upon your back; maybe you may dream.

FORESIGHT.

I thank you, Mr. Scandal, I will. Nurse, let me have a 565
watch-light, and lay the *Crumbs of Comfort* by me.

NURSE.

Yes, sir.

FORESIGHT.

And—hem, hem! I am very faint.

SCANDAL.

No, no, you look much better.

FORESIGHT [*to* Nurse].

Do I? And d'ye hear—bring me, let me see—within a 570
quarter of twelve—hem—he, hem!—just upon the turning
of the tide, bring me the urinal. And I hope neither the lord
of my ascendant nor the moon will be combust; and then I
may do well.

SCANDAL.

I hope so. Leave that to me; I will erect a scheme; and I 575
hope I shall find both Sol and Venus in the sixth house.

FORESIGHT.

I thank you, Mr. Scandal. Indeed, that would be a great
comfort to me. Hem, hem! Good night.   *Exit.*

SCANDAL.

Good night, good Mr. Foresight. And I hope Mars and
Venus will be in conjunction—while your wife and I are 580
together.

MRS. FORESIGHT.

Well, and what use do you hope to make of this project?

579.] SCENE XIV W1.

---

563. *diacodian and cowslip water*] syrup from poppy heads, used chiefly as
an opiate, and a medicinal from cowslips.

566. *Crumbs of Comfort*] a popular book of devotion.

573. *combust*] When a planet is within 8° 30′ of the body of the sun, its
astrological influence is destroyed.

576. *find . . . house*] in conjunction.

You don't think that you are ever like to succeed in your design upon me.

SCANDAL.

Yes, faith, I do; I have a better opinion both of you and 585
myself than to despair.

MRS. FORESIGHT.

Did you ever hear such a toad? Hark'ee, devil, do you
think any woman honest?

SCANDAL.

Yes, several, very honest; they'll cheat a little at cards,
sometimes, but that's nothing. 590

MRS. FORESIGHT.

Pshaw! but virtuous, I mean.

SCANDAL.

Yes, faith, I believe some women are virtuous too; but 'tis as
I believe some men are valiant, through fear. For why should
a man court danger or a woman shun pleasure?

MRS. FORESIGHT.

O monstrous! What are conscience and honor? 595

SCANDAL.

Why, honor is a public enemy, and conscience a domestic
thief; and he that would secure his pleasure must pay a
tribute to one, and go halves with the t'other. As for honor,
that you have secured, for you have purchased a perpetual
opportunity for pleasure. 600

MRS. FORESIGHT.

An opportunity for pleasure!

SCANDAL.

Aye, your husband; a husband is an opportunity for
pleasure, so you have taken care of honor, and 'tis the least
I can do to take care of conscience.

MRS. FORESIGHT.

And so you think we are free for one another? 605

SCANDAL.

Yes, faith, I think so; I love to speak my mind.

MRS. FORESIGHT.

Why, then, I'll speak my mind. Now as to this affair between
you and me. Here you make love to me; why, I'll confess it
does not displease me. Your person is well enough, and
your understanding is not amiss. 610

SCANDAL.

I have no great opinion of myself, yet I think I'm neither
deformed nor a fool.

MRS. FORESIGHT.

But you have a villainous character; you are a libertine in
speech as well as practice.

SCANDAL.

Come, I know what you would say. You think it more 615
dangerous to be seen in conversation with me than to allow
some other men the last favor. You mistake; the liberty I
take in talking is purely affected, for the service of your sex.
He that first cries out stop thief, is often he that has stolen
the treasure. I am a juggler that act by confederacy; and 620
if you please, we'll put a trick upon the world.

MRS. FORESIGHT.

Aye, but you are such a universal juggler that I'm afraid
you have a great many confederates.

SCANDAL.

Faith, I'm sound.

MRS. FORESIGHT.

O fie—I'll swear you're impudent.   625

SCANDAL.

I'll swear you're handsome.

MRS. FORESIGHT.

Pish, you'd tell me so, though you did not think so.

SCANDAL.

And you'd think so, though I should not tell you so; and
now I think we know one another pretty well.

MRS. FORESIGHT.

O Lord, who's here?   630

Enter Mrs. Frail *and* Ben.

BEN.

Mess, I love to speak my mind. Father has nothing to do
with me. Nay, I can't say that neither; he has something to
do with me. But what does that signify? If so be that I ben't
minded to be steered by him, 'tis as tho'f he should strive
against wind and tide.   635

630.1.] SCENE XV *W1.*

MRS. FRAIL.

Aye, but, my dear, we must keep it secret, till the estate be settled; for you know, marrying without an estate is like sailing in a ship without ballast.

BEN.

He, he, he, why, that's true; just so, for all the world it is indeed, as like as two cable ropes.   640

MRS. FRAIL.

And though I have a good portion, you know one would not venture all in one bottom.

BEN.

Why, that's true again; for mayhap one bottom may spring a leak. You have hit it indeed; mess, you've nicked the channel.   645

MRS. FRAIL.

Well, but if you should forsake me after all, you'd break my heart.

BEN.

Break your heart? I'd rather the Marygold should break her cable in a storm, as well as I love her. Flesh, you don't think I'm false-hearted, like a landman. A sailor will be honest, 650 tho'f mayhap he has never a penny of money in his pocket. Mayhap I may not have so fair a face as a citizen or a courtier, but for all that, I've as good blood in my veins and a heart as sound as a biscuit.

MRS. FRAIL.

And will you love me always?   655

BEN.

Nay, an I love once, I'll stick like pitch; I'll tell you that. Come, I'll sing you a song of a sailor.

MRS. FRAIL.

Hold, there's my sister; I'll call her to hear it.

MRS. FORESIGHT [to Scandal].

Well, I won't go to bed to my husband tonight, because I'll retire to my own chamber and think of what you have said. 660

SCANDAL.

Well, you'll give me leave to wait upon you to your chamber door, and leave you my last instructions?

---

642. *venture . . . bottom*] nautical language for placing all of one's resources in one speculation.

mrs. foresight.

Hold, here's my sister coming toward us.

mrs. frail.

If it won't interrupt you, I'll entertain you with a song.

ben.

The song was made upon one of our ship's crew's wife; our 665
boatswain made the song; mayhap you may know her, sir.
Before she was married, she was called Buxom Joan of
Deptford.

scandal.

I have heard of her.

Ben *sings.*

BALLAD
Set by Mr. John Eccles

A soldier and a sailor,   670
A tinker, and a tailor,
Had once a doubtful strife, sir,
To make a maid a wife, sir,
    Whose name was Buxom Joan.
For now the time was ended,   675
When she no more intended,
To lick her lips at men, sir,
And gnaw the sheets in vain, sir,
    And lie o'nights alone.

2.

The soldier swore like thunder,   680
He loved her more than plunder;
And showed her many a scar, sir,
That he had brought from far, sir,
    With fighting for her sake.
The tailor thought to please her,   685
With off'ring her his measure.
The tinker too with mettle,
Said he could mend her kettle,
    And stop up ev'ry leak.

3.

But while these three were prating,   690
The sailor slyly waiting,

> Thought if it came about, sir,
> That they should all fall out, sir;
>   He then might play his part.
> And just e'en as he meant, sir,   695
> To loggerheads they went, sir,
> And then he let fly at her,
> A shot 'twixt wind and water,
>   That won this fair maid's heart.

BEN.

If some of our crew that came to see me are not gone, you 700
shall see that we sailors can dance sometimes, as well as
other folks. (*Whistles.*) I warrant that brings 'em, an
they be within hearing.

Enter Seamen.

O, here they be. And fiddles along with 'em. Come, my lads,
let's have a round, and I'll make one.   *Dance.* 705
We're merry folk, we sailors; we han't much to care for.
Thus we live at sea, eat biscuit, and drink flip, put on a
clean shirt once a quarter. Come home and lie with our
landladies once a year, get rid of a little money, and then
put off with the next fair wind. How de'e like us?   710

MRS. FRAIL.

O, you are the happiest, merriest men alive.

MRS. FORESIGHT.

We're beholding to Mr. Benjamin for this entertainment.
I believe it's late.

BEN.

Why, forsooth, an you think so, you had best go to bed.
For my part, I mean to toss a can, and remember my 715
sweetheart, afore I turn in; mayhap I may dream of her.

MRS. FORESIGHT.

Mr. Scandal, you had best go to bed and dream too.

SCANDAL.

Why, faith, I have a good lively imagination, and can
dream as much to the purpose as another, if I set about it.
But dreaming is the poor retreat of a lazy, hopeless, and 720

---

707. *flip*] mixture of beer and spirit, sweetened and heated.
715. *toss a can*] take a drink.

imperfect lover; 'tis the last glimpse of love to worn-out sinners, and the faint dawning of a bliss to wishing girls and growing boys.

There's nought but willing, waking love, that can
Make blest the ripened maid and finished man.   725

Exeunt.

The End of the Third Act

ACT IV

Valentine's Lodging.
Enter Scandal *and* Jeremy.

SCANDAL.

Well, is your master ready? Does he look madly, and talk
madly?

JEREMY.

Yes, sir; you need make no great doubt of that. He that was
so near turning poet yesterday morning can't be much to
seek in playing the madman today.   5

SCANDAL.

Would he have Angelica acquainted with the reason of his
design?

JEREMY.

No, sir, not yet. He has a mind to try whether his playing
the madman won't make her play the fool, and fall in love
with him; or at least own that she has loved him all this   10
while and concealed it.

SCANDAL.

I saw her take coach just now with her maid, and think I
heard her bid the coachman drive hither.

JEREMY.

Like enough, sir, for I told her maid this morning, my
master was run stark mad only for love of her mistress. I   15
hear a coach stop; if it should be she, sir, I believe he would
not see her, till he hears how she takes it.

SCANDAL.

Well, I'll try her. —'Tis she, here she comes.

Enter Angelica *with* Jenny.

ANGELICA.

Mr. Scandal, I suppose you don't think it a novelty to see a
woman visit a man at his own lodgings in a morning?   20

SCANDAL.

Not upon a kind occasion, madam. But when a lady comes
tyrannically to insult a ruined lover and make manifest the

18.1.] SCENE II *W1*.

cruel triumphs of her beauty, the barbarity of it something
surprises me.

ANGELICA.

I don't like raillery from a serious face. Pray tell me what is   25
the matter?

JEREMY.

No strange matter, madam. My master's mad, that's all;
I suppose your ladyship has thought him so a great while.

ANGELICA.

How d'ye mean, mad?

JEREMY.

Why, faith, madam, he's mad for want of his wits, just as he   30
was poor for want of money. His head is e'en as light as his
pockets, and anybody that has a mind to a bad bargain
can't do better than to beg him for his estate.

ANGELICA.

If you speak truth, your endeavoring at wit is very unseasonable—   35

SCANDAL (*aside*).

She's concerned, and loves him.

ANGELICA.

Mr. Scandal, you can't think me guilty of so much in-
humanity, as not to be concerned for a man I must own
myself obliged to—pray tell me truth.

SCANDAL.

Faith, madam, I wish telling a lie would mend the matter.   40
But this is no new effect of an unsuccessful passion.

ANGELICA (*aside*).

I know not what to think. Yet I should be vexed to have a
trick put upon me. —May I not see him?

SCANDAL.

I'm afraid the physician is not willing you should see him
yet. Jeremy, go in and inquire.   *Exit* Jeremy.   45

ANGELICA [*aside*].

Ha! I saw him wink and smile. I fancy 'tis a trick! I'll try.
—I would disguise to all the world a failing, which I must
own to you. I fear my happiness depends upon the recovery
of Valentine. Therefore, I conjure you, as you are his friend

46]. SCENE III *WI.*

and as you have compassion upon one fearful of affliction, to 50
tell me what I am to hope for. I cannot speak. But you may
tell me, for you know what I would ask?

SCANDAL [*aside*].

So, this is pretty plain. —Be not too much concerned,
madam; I hope his condition is not desperate. An acknowledgment of love from you, perhaps, may work a cure, as 55
the fear of your aversion occasioned his distemper.

ANGELICA (*aside*).

Say you so; nay, then, I'm convinced. And if I don't play
trick for trick, may I never taste the pleasure of revenge.
—Acknowledgment of love! I find you have mistaken my
compassion, and think me guilty of a weakness I am a 60
stranger to. But I have too much sincerity to deceive you
and too much charity to suffer him to be deluded with vain
hopes. Good nature and humanity oblige me to be concerned for him, but to love is neither in my power nor
inclination; and if he can't be cured without I suck the 65
poison from his wounds, I'm afraid he won't recover his
senses till I lose mine.

SCANDAL.

Hey, brave woman, i'faith—won't you see him then, if
he desire it?

ANGELICA.

What signify a madman's desires? Besides, 'twould make me 70
uneasy. If I don't see him, perhaps my concern for him may
lessen. If I forget him, 'tis no more than he has done by
himself. And now the surprise is over, methinks I am not
half so sorry for him as I was.

SCANDAL.

So, faith, good nature works apace. You were confessing 75
just now an obligation to his love.

ANGELICA.

But I have considered that passions are unreasonable and
involuntary. If he loves, he can't help it; and if I don't love,
I can't help it; no more than he can help his being a man,
or I my being a woman; or no more than I can help my 80
want of inclination to stay longer here. Come, Jenny.

Exit Angelica *and* Jenny.

SCANDAL.

Humh! An admirable composition, faith, this same woman-
kind.

Enter Jeremy.

JEREMY.

What, is she gone, sir?

SCANDAL.

Gone! Why, she was never here, nor anywhere else; nor I   85
don't know her if I see her, nor you neither.

JEREMY.

Good lack! What's the matter now? Are any more of us to be
mad? Why, sir, my master longs to see her, and is almost
mad in good earnest, with the joyful news of her being here.

SCANDAL.

We are all under a mistake. Ask no questions, for I can't   90
resolve you, but I'll inform your master. In the meantime,
if our project succeed no better with his father than it does
with his mistress, he may descend from his exaltation of
madness into the road of common sense, and be content only
to be made a fool with other reasonable people. I hear Sir   95
Sampson. You know your cue; I'll to your master.   *Exit.*

Enter Sir Sampson *with a lawyer.*

SIR SAMPSON.

D'ye see, Mr. Buckram, here's the paper signed with his
own hand.

BUCKRAM.

Good, sir. And the conveyance is ready drawn in this box,
if he be ready to sign and seal.   100

SIR SAMPSON.

Ready, body o'me, he must be ready. His sham sickness
shan't excuse him. O, here's his scoundrel. Sirrah, where's
your master?

JEREMY.

Ah, sir, he's quite gone.

SIR SAMPSON.

Gone! What, he is not dead?   105

82.] SCENE IV *W1.*   96.1.] SCENE V *W1.*

JEREMY.

No, sir, not dead.

SIR SAMPSON.

What, is he gone out of town, run away, ha! Has he tricked me? Speak, varlet.

JEREMY.

No, no, sir, he's safe enough, sir, an he were but as sound, poor gentleman. He is indeed here, sir, and not here, sir.   110

SIR SAMPSON.

Hey day, rascal, do you banter me? Sirrah, d'ye banter me? Speak, sirrah, where is he, for I will find him.

JEREMY.

Would you could, sir, for he has lost himself. Indeed, sir, I have almost broke my heart about him. I can't refrain tears when I think of him, sir; I'm as melancholy for him as   115 a passing-bell, sir, or a horse in a pound.

SIR SAMPSON.

A pox confound your similitudes, sir. Speak to be understood, and tell me in plain terms what the matter is with him, or I'll crack your fool's skull.

JEREMY.

Ah, you've hit it, sir; that's the matter with him, sir. His   120 skull's cracked, poor gentleman; he's stark mad, sir.

SIR SAMPSON.

Mad!

BUCKRAM.

What, is he *non compos*?

JEREMY.

Quite *non compos*, sir.

BUCKRAM.

Why, then all's obliterated, Sir Sampson. If he be *non*   125 *compos mentis*, his act and deed will be of no effect; it is not good in law.

SIR SAMPSON.

Oons, I won't believe it; let me see him, sir. Mad—I'll make him find his senses.

JEREMY.

Mr. Scandal is with him, sir; I'll knock at the door.   130

---

116. *pound*] an enclosure, possibly a pond.

Goes to the scene, which opens and discovers Valentine *upon a couch disorderly dressed*, Scandal *by him*.

SIR SAMPSON.

How now, what's here to do?

VALENTINE.

Ha! Who's that? *Starting.*

SCANDAL.

For heaven's sake, softly, sir, and gently; don't provoke him.

VALENTINE.

Answer me. Who is that? and that?

SIR SAMPSON.

Gads bobs, does he not know me? Is he mischievous? I'll 135
speak gently. Val, Val, dost thou not know me, boy? Not
know thy own father, Val! I am thy own father, and this is
honest Brief Buckram the lawyer.

VALENTINE.

It may be so—I did not know you—the world is full—
There are people that we do know, and people that we do 140
not know; and yet the sun shines upon all alike. There are
fathers that have many children, and there are children
that have many fathers. 'Tis strange! But I am Truth, and
come to give the world the lie.

SIR SAMPSON.

Body o'me, I know not what to say to him. 145

VALENTINE.

Why does that lawyer wear black? Does he carry his
conscience withoutside? Lawyer, what are thou? Dost thou
know me?

BUCKRAM.

O Lord, what must I say? Yes, sir.

VALENTINE.

Thou liest, for I am Truth. 'Tis hard I cannot get a live- 150
lihood amongst you. I have been sworn out of Westminster
Hall the first day of every term. Let me see—no matter how
long. But I'll tell you one thing; it's a question that would
puzzle an arithmetician, if you should ask him, whether the

130.1.] SCENE VI *W1.*

---

135. *mischievous*] out of his mind, possibly dangerous.
152. *term*] a judicial session at Westminster Hall.

Bible saves more souls in Westminster Abbey, or damns more   155
in Westminster Hall. For my part, I am Truth, and can't
tell; I have very few acquaintance.

SIR SAMPSON.

Body o'me, he talks sensibly in his madness. Has he no
intervals?

JEREMY.

Very short, sir.   160

BUCKRAM.

Sir, I can do you no service while he's in this condition.
Here's your paper, sir. He may do me a mischief if I stay.
The conveyance is ready, sir, if he recover his senses.   *Exit.*

SIR SAMPSON.

Hold, hold, don't you go yet.

SCANDAL.

You'd better let him go, sir, and send for him if there be   165
occasion, for I fancy his presence provokes him more.

VALENTINE.

Is the lawyer gone? 'Tis well, then we may drink about
without going together by the ears. Heigh ho! What o'clock
is't? My father here! Your blessing, sir?

SIR SAMPSON.

He recovers. Bless thee, Val. How dost thou do, boy?   170

VALENTINE.

Thank you, sir, pretty well. I have been a little out of order.
Won't you please to sit, sir?

SIR SAMPSON.

Aye, boy. Come, thou shalt sit down by me.

VALENTINE.

Sir, 'tis my duty to wait.

SIR SAMPSON.

No, no, come, come, sit you down, honest Val. How dost   175
thou do? Let me feel thy pulse. O, pretty well now, Val.
Body o'me, I was sorry to see thee indisposed, but I'm glad
thou'rt better, honest Val.

VALENTINE.

I thank you, sir.

164.] SCENE VII *Wl.*

---

168. *going . . . ears*] being at variance, like dogs biting other dogs' ears.

SCANDAL *(aside)*.

Miracle! the monster grows loving.   180

SIR SAMPSON.

Let me feel thy hand again, Val. It does not shake; I believe
thou canst write, Val. Ha, boy? Thou canst write thy name,
Val? [*In a whisper to Jeremy.*] Jeremy, step and overtake
Mr. Buckram; bid him haste back with the conveyance—
quick—quick.   *Exit* Jeremy. 185

SCANDAL *(aside)*.

That ever I should suspect such a heathen of any remorse.

SIR SAMPSON.

Dost thou know this paper, Val; I know thou'rt honest and
wilt perform articles.

> *Shows him the paper, but holds it out of his reach.*

VALENTINE.

Pray let me see it, sir. You hold it so far off that I can't tell
whether I know it or no.   190

SIR SAMPSON.

See it, boy? Aye, aye, why thou dost see it; 'tis thy own
hand, Val. Why, let me see, I can read it as plain as can be.
Look you here. (*Reads.*)   *The condition of this obligation*—
Look you, as plain as can be, so it begins. And than at the
bottom, *As witness my hand*, VALENTINE LEGEND, in 195
great letters. Why, 'tis as plain as the nose in one's face.
What, are my eyes better than thine? I believe I can read it
farther off yet—let me see.

> *Stretches his arm as far as he can.*

VALENTINE.

Will you please to let me hold it, sir?

SIR SAMPSON.

Let thee hold it, sayst thou. Aye, with all my heart. What 200
matter is it who holds it? What need anybody hold it? I'll
put it up in my pocket, Val, and then nobody need hold it.
(*Puts the paper in his pocket.*)   There, Val, it's safe enough,
boy. But thou shalt have it as soon as thou has set thy hand
to another paper, little Val.   205

> *Re-enter* Jeremy *with* Buckram.

186.] SCENE VIII *W1*.   205.1.] SCENE IX *W1*.

VALENTINE.

What, is my bad genius here again! O no, 'tis the lawyer with an itching palm, and he's come to be scratched. My nails are not long enough. Let me have a pair of red-hot tongs quickly, quickly, and you shall see me act St. Dunstan, and lead the devil by the nose.   210

BUCKRAM.

O Lord, let me be gone; I'll not venture myself with a madman.   *Exit* Buckram.

VALENTINE.

Ha, ha, ha, you need not run so fast; honesty will not overtake you. Ha, ha, ha, the rogue found me out to be in *forma pauperis* presently.   215

SIR SAMPSON.

Ooons! What a vexation is here! I know not what to do, or say, nor which way to go.

VALENTINE.

Who's that, that's out of his way?—I am Truth, and can set him right. Harkee, friend, the straight road is the worst way you can go. He that follows his nose always will very 220 often be led into a stink. *Probatum est.* But what are you for? Religion or politics? There's a couple of topics for you, no more like one another than oil and vinegar, and yet those two beaten together by a state-cook make sauce for the whole nation.   225

SIR SAMPSON.

What the devil had I to do, ever to beget sons? Why did I ever marry?

VALENTINE.

Because thou wert a monster, old boy? The two greatest monsters in the world are a man and a woman. What's thy opinion?   230

SIR SAMPSON.

Why, my opinion is that those two monsters joined together make yet a greater, that's a man and his wife.

213.] SCENE X *W1*.

209–210. *St. Dunstan . . . nose*] St. Dunstan is said to have caught the devil by the nose with pliers when the devil tried to tempt him.

VALENTINE.

>Aha! Old truepenny, sayst thou so? Thou hast nicked it.
>But it's wonderful strange, Jeremy.

JEREMY.

>What is, sir?   235

VALENTINE.

>That gray hairs should cover a green head—and I make a
>fool of my father.

>*Enter* Foresight, Mrs. Foresight, *and* Mrs. Frail.

>What's here? *Erra pater*? Or a bearded sybil? If Prophecy
>comes, Truth must give place.   *Exit with* Jeremy.

FORESIGHT.

>What says he? What, did he prophesy? Ha, Sir Sampson, 240
>bless us! How are we?

SIR SAMPSON.

>Are we? An, pox o' your prognostication. Why, we are fools
>as we use to be. Oons, that you could not foresee that the
>moon would predominate, and my son be mad. Where's
>your oppositions, your trines, and your quadrates? What 245
>did your Cardan and your Ptolemy tell you? Your Messa-
>halah and your Longomontanus, your harmony of chiro-
>mancy with astrology. Ah! pox on't, that I that know the
>world, and men and manners, that don't believe a syllable
>in the sky and stars, and sun and almanacs, and trash, 250
>should be directed by a dreamer, an omen-hunter, and
>defer business in expectation of a lucky hour. When, body
>o'me, there never was a lucky hour after the first opportunity.

>   *Exit* Sir Sampson.

FORESIGHT.

>Ah, Sir Sampson, heaven help your head. This is none of
>your lucky hour. *Nemo omnibus horis sapit.* What, is he gone, 255
>and in contempt of science! Ill stars and unconverted
>ignorance attend him.

240.] SCENE XI *W1*.   254.] SCENE XII *W1*.

---

238. *Erra pater*] nickname for an old astrologer or his almanac.
246. *Cardan*] Girolamo Cardan, Italian occultist of the sixteenth century.
247. *Longomontanus*] a Dutch astronomer of the sixteenth century.
255. *Nemo . . . sapit*] No one is wise at all times.

SCANDAL.

> You must excuse his passion, Mr. Foresight, for he has been
> heartily vexed. His son is *non compos mentis*, and thereby
> incapable of making any conveyance in law, so that all his 260
> measures are disappointed.

FORESIGHT.

> Ha! say you so?

MRS. FRAIL (*aside to* Mrs. Foresight).

> What, has my sea-lover lost his anchor of hope then?

MRS. FORESIGHT.

> O sister, what will you do with him?

MRS. FRAIL.

> Do with him? Send him to sea again in the next foul 265
> weather. He's used to an inconstant element, and won't be
> surprised to see the tide turned.

FORESIGHT (*considers*).

> Wherein was I mistaken, not to foresee this?

SCANDAL (*aside to* Mrs. Foresight).

> Madam, you and I can tell him something else that he did
> not foresee, and more particularly relating to his own fortune. 270

MRS. FORESIGHT.

> What do you mean? I don't understand you.

SCANDAL.

> Hush, softly, the pleasures of last night, my dear, too
> considerable to be forgot so soon.

MRS. FORESIGHT.

> Last night! And what would your impudence infer from last
> night? Last night was like the night before, I think.   275

SCANDAL.

> 'Sdeath, do you make no difference between me and your
> husband?

MRS. FORESIGHT.

> Not much. He's superstitious, and you are mad, in my
> opinion.

SCANDAL.

> You make me mad. You are not serious. Pray recollect 280
> yourself.

MRS. FORESIGHT.

> O yes, now I remember. You were very impertinent and
> impudent, and would have come to bed to me.

SCANDAL.

And did not?

MRS. FORESIGHT.

Did not! With that face can you ask the question?   285

SCANDAL.

This I have heard of before but never believed. I have been
told she had that admirable quality of forgetting to a man's
face in the morning that she had lain with him all night,
and denying favors with more impudence than she could
grant 'em. Madam, I'm your humble servant and honor   290
you. You look pretty well, Mr. Foresight. How did you rest
last night?

FORESIGHT.

Truly, Mr. Scandal, I was so taken up with broken dreams
and distracted visions that I remember little.

SCANDAL.

'Twas a very forgetting night. But would you not talk with   295
Valentine, perhaps you may understand him; I'm apt to
believe there is something mysterious in his discourses, and
sometimes rather think him inspired than mad.

FORESIGHT.

You speak with singular good judgment, Mr. Scandal, truly.
I am inclining to your Turkish opinion in this matter, and   300
do reverence a man whom the vulgar think mad. Let us go
in to him.

MRS. FRAIL.

Sister, do you stay with them; I'll find out my lover and
give him his discharge, and come to you. O'my conscience,
here he comes.   305

Exeunt Foresight, Mrs. Foresight, *and* Scandal.

Enter Ben.

BEN.

All mad, I think. Flesh, I believe all the calentures of the
sea are come ashore, for my part.

MRS. FRAIL.

Mr. Benjamin in choler!

301–302. go in to] *Q1–4*; go to *W1*.   305.2.] SCENE XIII *W1*.

306. *calentures*] diseases or fevers contracted by sailors.

BEN.

No, I'm pleased well enough, now I have found you. Mess,
I have had such a hurricane upon your account yonder.   310

MRS. FRAIL.

My account, pray what's the matter?

BEN.

Why, father came and found me squabbling with yon
chitty-faced thing, as he would have me marry; so he asked
what was the matter. He asked in a surly sort of way. (It
seems brother Val is gone mad, and so that put'n into a   315
passion; but what did I know that, what's that to me?)
So he asked in a surly sort of manner, and gad I answered'n
as surlily. What thof' he be my father, I an't bound prentice
to 'en. So faith, I told'n in plain terms, if I were minded to
marry, I'de marry to please myself, not him; and for the 320
young woman that he provided for me, I thought it more
fitting for her to learn her sampler, and make dirt-pies, than
to look after a husband; for my part I was none of her man.
I had another voyage to make; let him take it as he will.

MRS. FRAIL.

So then you intend to go to sea again?   325

BEN.

Nay, nay, my mind run upon you, but I would not tell him
so much. So he said he'd make my heart ache, and if so be
that he could get a woman to his mind, he'd marry himself.
Gad, says I, an you play the fool and marry at these years,
there's more danger of your head's aching than my heart. 330
He was woundy angry when I gav'n that wipe. He hadn't a
word to say, and so I left'n, and the green girl together.
Mayhap the bee may bite, and he'll marry her himself, with
all my heart.

MRS. FRAIL.

And were you this undutiful and graceless wretch to your 335
father?

BEN.

Then why was he graceless first? If I am undutiful and
graceless, why did he beget me so? I did not get myself.

317. answer'd'n] Q1–3; answer'd'en
Q4, W1.

MRS. FRAIL.

O impiety! How have I been mistaken! What an inhuman merciless creature have I set my heart upon? O, I am 340 happy to have discovered the shelves and quicksands that lurk beneath that faithless smiling face.

BEN.

Hey toss! What's the matter now? Why, you ben't angry, be you?

MRS. FRAIL.

O see me no more, for thou wert born amongst rocks, 345 suckled by whales, cradled in a tempest, and whistled to by winds; and thou art come forth with fins and scales, and three rows of teeth, a most outrageous fish of prey.

BEN.

O Lord, O Lord, she's mad, poor young woman. Love has turned her senses; her brain is quite overset. Well-a-day, 350 how shall I do to set her to rights?

MRS. FRAIL.

No, no, I am not mad, monster; I am wise enough to find you out. Hadst thou the impudence to aspire at being a husband with that stubborn and disobedient temper? You that know not how to submit to a father, presume to have a 355 sufficient stock of duty to undergo a wife? I should have been finely fobbed, indeed, very finely fobbed.

BEN.

Hark'ee forsooth, if so be that you are in your right senses, d'ee see; for aught as I perceive I'm like to be finely fobbed —if I have got anger here upon your account, and you are 360 tacked about already. What d'ee mean, after all your fair speeches, and stroking my cheeks, and kissing and hugging, what, would you sheer off so? Would you, and leave me aground?

MRS. FRAIL.

No, I'll leave you adrift, and go which way you will. 365

BEN.

What, are you false-hearted then?

MRS. FRAIL.

Only the wind's changed.

BEN.

More shame for you—the wind's changed? It's an ill wind

blows nobody good. Mayhap I have good riddance on you,
if these be your tricks. What d'ee mean all this while, to 370
make a fool of me?

MRS. FRAIL.

Any fool but a husband.

BEN.

Husband! Gad, I would not be your husband, if you would
have me, now I know your mind, thof' you had your weight
in gold and jewels, and thof' I loved you never so well.   375

MRS. FRAIL.

Why, canst thou love, porpoise?

BEN.

No matter what I can do, don't call names—I don't love you
so well as to bear that, whatever I did. I'm glad you show
yourself, mistress. Let them marry you, as don't know you.
Gad, I know you too well, by sad experience; I believe he 380
that marries you will go to sea in a hen-pecked frigate. I
believe that, young woman, and mayhap may come to an
anchor at Cuckold's Point; so there's a dash for you, take it
as you will. Mayhap you may holla after me when I won't
come too.   *Exit.* 385

MRS. FRAIL.

Ha, ha, ha, no doubt on't. —(*Sings.*) *My true love is gone
to sea*—

                    Enter Mrs. Foresight.

O sister, had you come a minute sooner, you would have
seen the resolution of a lover. Honest Tar and I are parted,
and with the same indifference that we met. O'my life, I am 390
half vexed at the insensibility of a brute that I despised.

MRS. FORESIGHT.

What then, he bore it most heroically?

MRS. FRAIL.

Most tyrannically, for you see he has got the start of me, and
I, the poor forsaken maid, am left complaining on the shore.
But I'll tell you a hint that he has given me. Sir Sampson is 395

375. thof'] *Q1–2, Q4*; tho'f *Q3, W1.*   387.1.] SCENE XIV *W1.*

383. *Cuckold's Point*] a place on the Thames, with an obvious pun on the
name.
383. *dash*] thrust or prophecy.

enraged, and talks desperately of committing matrimony
himself. If he has a mind to throw himself away, he can't do
it more effectually than upon me, if we could bring it about.

MRS. FORESIGHT.

O hang him, old fox; he's too cunning; besides, he hates
both you and me. But I have a project in my head for you, 400
and I have gone a good way towards it. I have almost made
a bargain with Jeremy, Valentine's man, to sell his master
to us.

MRS. FRAIL.

Sell him, how?

MRS. FORESIGHT.

Valentine raves upon Angelica, and took me for her, and 405
Jeremy says will take anybody for her that he imposes on
him. Now I have promised him mountains, if in one of his
mad fits he will bring you to him in her stead, and get you
married together, and put to bed together, and after
consummation, girl, there's no revoking. And if he should 410
recover his senses, he'll be glad at least to make you a good
settlement. Here they come, stand aside a little, and tell me
how you like the design.

Enter Valentine, Scandal, Foresight, *and* Jeremy.

SCANDAL (*to* Jeremy).

And have you given your master a hint of their plot upon
him?   415

JEREMY.

Yes, sir. He says he'll favor it, and mistake her for Angelica.

SCANDAL.

It may make sport.

FORESIGHT.

Mercy on us!

VALENTINE.

Hush, interrupt me not—I'll whisper prediction to thee,
and thou shalt prophesy. I am Truth, and can teach thy 420
tongue a new trick. I have told thee what's past; now I tell
what's to come. Dost thou know what will happen tomorrow? Answer me not, for I will tell thee. Tomorrow

413.1.] SCENE XV *W1.*

knaves will thrive through craft, and fools through fortune,
and honesty will go as it did, frost-nipped in a summer suit. 425
Ask me questions concerning tomorrow?

SCANDAL.

Ask him, Mr. Foresight.

FORESIGHT.

Pray, what will be done at court?

VALENTINE.

Scandal will tell you; I am Truth, I never come there.

FORESIGHT.

In the City?   430

VALENTINE.

O, prayers will be said in empty churches at the usual
hours. Yet you will see such zealous faces behind counters,
as if religion were to be sold in every shop. O, things will go
methodically in the City. The clocks will strike twelve at
noon, and the horned herd buzz in the Exchange at two. 435
Wives and husbands will drive distinct trades, and care and
pleasure separately occupy the family. Coffeehouses will be
full of smoke and stratagem. And the cropt prentice, that
sweeps his master's shop in the morning, may, ten to one,
dirty his sheets before night. But there are two things that 440
you will see very strange, which are wanton wives, with their
legs at liberty, and tame cuckolds, with chains about their
necks. But hold, I must examine you before I go further.
You look suspiciously. Are you a husband?

FORESIGHT.

I am married.   445

VALENTINE.

Poor creature! Is your wife of Covent Garden parish?

FORESIGHT.

No, St. Martin's-in-the-Fields.

VALENTINE.

Alas, poor man; his eyes are sunk, and his hands shriveled;
his legs dwindled, and his back bowed. Pray, pray, for a
metamorphosis. Change thy shape, and shake off age. Get 450
thee Medea's kettle, and be boiled anew. Come forth with

---

435. *Exchange*] the New Exchange in the Strand.
451. *Medea's . . . anew*] Medea by her magic cauldron restored youth
to Jason's father.

laboring callous hands, a chine of steel, and Atlas shoulders.
Let Taliacotius trim the calves of twenty chairmen, and
make thee pedestals to stand erect upon, and look matrimony
in the face. Ha, ha, ha! That a man should have a stomach 455
to a wedding supper, when the pigeons ought rather to be
laid to his feet, ha, ha, ha.

FORESIGHT [*oblivious of the plot*].
His frenzy is very high now, Mr. Scandal.

SCANDAL.
I believe it is a spring tide.

FORESIGHT.
Very likely, truly. You understand these matters. Mr. 460
Scandal, I shall be very glad to confer with you about these
things which he has uttered. His sayings are very mysterious
and hieroglyphical.

VALENTINE.
O, why would Angelica be absent from my eyes so long?

JEREMY.
She's here, sir.   465

MRS. FORESIGHT.
Now, sister.

MRS. FRAIL.
O Lord, what must I say?

SCANDAL.
Humor him, madam, by all means.

VALENTINE.
Where is she? O, I see her. She comes, like riches, health,
and liberty at once, to a despairing, starving, and abandoned 470
wretch. O welcome, welcome.

MRS. FRAIL.
How de'e you, sir? Can I serve you?

VALENTINE.
Harkee, I have a secret to tell you. Endymion and the moon
shall meet us upon Mount Latmos, and we'll be married in

---

452. *chine*] backbone.
453. *Taliacotius*] a sixteenth-century surgeon.
456–457. *pigeons . . . feet*] a remedy administered by applying hot bricks
to the feet, then a live pigeon cut in two parts.
473. *Endymion*] a beautiful youth granted eternal youthfulness through
eternal sleep.
474. *Latmos*] legendary mountain where Endymion pastured his flocks.

the dead of night. But say not a word. Hymen shall put his 475
torch into a dark lanthorn, that it may be secret; and Juno
shall give her peacock poppy-water, that he may fold his
ogling tail, and Argos's hundred eyes be shut, ha? Nobody
shall know but Jeremy.

MRS. FRAIL.

No, no, we'll keep it secret; it shall be done presently.   480

VALENTINE.

The sooner the better. Jeremy, come hither—closer—that
none may overhear us. Jeremy, I can tell you news. Angelica
is turned nun, and I am turning friar, and yet we'll marry
one another in spite of the Pope. Get me a cowl and beads
that I may play my part, for she'll meet me two hours hence 485
in black and white, and a long veil to cover the project, and
we won't see one another's faces till we have done something
to be ashamed of, and then we'll blush once for all.

Enter Tattle *and* Angelica.

JEREMY.

I'll take care, and—

VALENTINE.

Whisper.   490

ANGELICA.

Nay, Mr. Tattle, if you make love to me, you spoil my
design, for I intended to make you my confidant.

TATTLE.

But, madam, to throw away your person, such a person!
and such a fortune, on a madman!

ANGELICA.

I never loved him till he was mad, but don't tell anybody so. 495

SCANDAL.

How's this! Tattle making love to Angelica!

TATTLE.

Tell, Madam! Alas, you don't know me. I have much ado
to tell your ladyship how long I have been in love with you,
but encouraged by the impossibility of Valentine's making

488.1.] SCENE XVI *W1.*

476–478. *Juno . . . shut*] Argos's hundred eyes were placed in the tail of
the peacock; Juno, personification of the genius of womanhood, will put
an opiate or soporific over the peacock; i.e., all shall be in secret.

any more addresses to you, I have ventured to declare the 500
very inmost passion of my heart. O, madam, look upon us
both. There you see the ruins of a poor decayed creature.
Here, a complete and lively figure, with youth and health,
and all his five senses in perfection, madam, and to all this,
the most passionate lover—   505

ANGELICA.

O fie for shame, hold your tongue. A passionate lover,
and five senses in perfection! When you are as mad as
Valentine, I'll believe you love me, and the maddest shall
take me.

VALENTINE.

It is enough. Ha! Who's here?   510

MRS. FRAIL (*to* Jeremy).

O Lord, her coming will spoil all.

JEREMY.

No, no, madam, he won't know her; if he should, I can
persuade him.

VALENTINE.

Scandal, who are all these? Foreigners? If they are, I'll
tell you what I think. (*Whisper.*) Get away all the 515
company but Angelica, that I may discover my design to
her.

SCANDAL.

I will. I have discovered something of Tattle, that is of a
piece with Mrs. Frail. He courts Angelica, if we could
contrive to couple 'em together. Harkee.   *Whisper.* 520

MRS. FORESIGHT.

He won't know you, cousin; he knows nobody.

FORESIGHT.

But he knows more than anybody. O, niece, he knows
things past and to come, and all the profound secrets of time.

TATTLE.

Look you, Mr. Foresight, it is not my way to make many
words of matters, and so I shan't say much, but in short, 525
de'e see, I will hold you a hundred pound now that I know
more secrets than he.

FORESIGHT.

How! I cannot read that knowledge in your face, Mr.
Tattle. Pray, what do you know?

TATTLE.

Why de'e think I'll tell you, sir? Read it in my face; no, sir, 530
'tis written in my heart. And safer there, sir, than letters
writ in juice of lemon, for no fire can fetch it out. I am no
blab, sir.

VALENTINE (*to* Scandal).

Acquaint Jeremy with it; he may easily bring it about.
—They are welcome, and I'll tell 'em so myself. What, do 535
you look strange upon me? Then I must be plain.   (*Coming
up to them.*)   I am Truth, and hate an old acquaintance
with a new face.   Scandal *goes aside with* Jeremy.

TATTLE.

Do you know me, Valentine?

VALENTINE.

You? Who are you? No, I hope not.   540

TATTLE.

I am Jack Tattle, your friend.

VALENTINE.

My friend, what to do? I am no married man, and thou
canst not lie with my wife. I am very poor, and thou canst
not borrow money of me. Then what employment have I
for a friend?   545

TATTLE.

Hah! A good open speaker, and not to be trusted with a
secret.

ANGELICA.

Do you know me, Valentine?

VALENTINE.

O, very well.

ANGELICA.

Who am I?   550

VALENTINE.

You're a woman, one to whom heaven gave beauty when it
grafted roses on a briar. You are the reflection of heaven in
a pond, and he that leaps at you is sunk. You are all white,
a sheet of lovely spotless paper, when you first are born, but
you are to be scrawled and blotted by every goose's quill. 555
I know you, for I loved a woman and loved her so long that
I found out a strange thing: I found out what a woman was
good for.

TATTLE.

Aye, prithee, what's that?

VALENTINE.

Why, to keep a secret.   560

TATTLE.

O Lord!

VALENTINE.

O exceeding good to keep a secret, for though she should
tell, yet she is not to be believed.

TATTLE.

Hah! good again, faith.

VALENTINE.

I would have music. Sing me the song that I like.   565

SONG

Set by Mr. Finger

1.

I tell thee, Charmion, could I time retrieve,
And could again begin to love and live,
To you I should my earliest off'ring give;
    I know my eyes would lead my heart to you,
    And I should all my vows and oaths renew,   570
    But to be plain, I never would be true.

2.

For by our weak and weary truth, I find,
Love hates to center on a point assigned,
But runs with joy the circle of the mind.
    Then never let us chain what should be free,   575
    But for relief of either sex agree,
    Since women love to change, and so do we.

VALENTINE (*walks musing*).

No more, for I am melancholy.

JEREMY (*to* Scandal).

I'll do't, sir.

SCANDAL.

Mr. Foresight, we had best leave him. He may grow out-   580
rageous and do mischief.

565.2. *Mr. Finger*] Godfrey [Gottfried] Finger, a contemporary composer.

FORESIGHT.

    I will be directed by you.

JEREMY (*to* Mrs. Frail).

    You'll meet, madam. I'll take care everything shall be ready.

MRS. FRAIL.

    Thou shalt do what thou wilt, have what thou wilt; in 585 short, I will deny thee nothing.

TATTLE (*to* Angelica).

    Madam, shall I wait upon you?

ANGELICA.

    No, I'll stay with him. Mr. Scandal will protect me. Aunt, Mr. Tattle desires you would give him leave to wait on you.

TATTLE [*aside*].

    Pox on't, there's no coming off, now she has said that. 590 —Madam, will you do me the honor?

MRS. FORESIGHT.

    Mr. Tattle might have used less ceremony.

        Exeunt Foresight, Mrs. Foresight, Tattle, Mrs. Frail, Jeremy.

SCANDAL.

    Jeremy, follow Tattle.

ANGELICA.

    Mr. Scandal, I only stay till my maid comes, and because I had a mind to be rid of Mr. Tattle.   595

SCANDAL.

    Madam, I am very glad that I overheard a better reason, which you gave to Mr. Tattle, for his impertinence forced you to acknowledge a kindness for Valentine, which you denied to all his sufferings and my solicitations. So I'll leave him to make use of the discovery, and your ladyship to the 600 free confession of your inclinations.

ANGELICA.

    O Heavens! You won't leave me alone with a madman?

SCANDAL.

    No, madam, I only leave a madman to his remedy.

        Exit Scandal.

593.] SCENE XVII *W1.*

VALENTINE.

    Madam, you need not be very much afraid, for I fancy I
begin to come to myself. 605

ANGELICA (*aside*).

    Aye, but if I don't fit you, I'll be hanged.

VALENTINE.

    You see what disguises love makes us put on. Gods have
been in counterfeited shapes for the same reason, and the
divine part of me, my mind, has worn this mask of madness,
and this motley livery, only as the slave of love, and menial 610
creature of your beauty.

ANGELICA.

    Mercy on me, how he talks! Poor Valentine!

VALENTINE.

    Nay, faith, now let us understand one another, hypocrisy
apart. The comedy draws toward an end, and let us think
of leaving acting and be ourselves; and since you have loved 615
me, you must own I have at length deserved you should
confess it.

ANGELICA (*sighs*).

    I would I had loved you, for heaven knows I pity you, and
could I have foreseen the sad effects, I would have striven;
but that's too late. 620

VALENTINE.

    What sad effects? What's too late? My seeming madness
has deceived my father and procured me time to think of
means to reconcile me to him and preserve the right of my
inheritance to his estate, which otherwise by articles I must
this morning have resigned. And this I had informed you of 625
today, but you were gone before I knew you had been here.

ANGELICA.

    How! I thought your love of me had caused this transport
in your soul, which, it seems, you only counterfeited for by
mercenary ends and sordid interest.

VALENTINE.

    Nay, now you do me wrong, for if any interest was 630

604.] SCENE XVIII *W1*.

---

606. *fit*] play an equally fine deception.

considered, it was yours, since I thought I wanted more
than love to make me worthy of you.

ANGELICA.

Then you thought me mercenary. But how am I deluded by
this interval of sense, to reason with a madman?

VALENTINE.

O, 'tis barbarous to misunderstand me longer.   635

Enter Jeremy.

ANGELICA.

O, here's a reasonable creature. Sure he will not have the
impudence to persevere. Come, Jeremy, acknowledge your
trick, and confess your master's madness counterfeit.

JEREMY.

Counterfeit, madam! I'll maintain him to be as absolutely
and substantially mad as any freeholder in Bethlehem. Nay,   640
he's as mad as any projector, fanatic, chemist, lover, or
poet in Europe.

VALENTINE.

Sirrah, you lie. I am not mad.

ANGELICA.

Ha, ha, ha, you see he denies it.

JEREMY.

O Lord, madam, did you ever know any madman mad   645
enough to own it?

VALENTINE.

Sot, can't you apprehend?

ANGELICA.

Why, he talked very sensibly just now.

JEREMY.

Yes, madam, he has intervals, but you see he begins to look
wild again.   650

VALENTINE.

Why, you thick-skulled rascal, I tell you the farce is done,
and I will be mad no longer.   *Beats him.*

ANGELICA.

Ha, ha, ha, is he mad, or no, Jeremy?

635.1.] SCENE XIX *W1.*

---

640. *Bethlehem*] Bedlam, the hospital for the insane.

JEREMY.

>Partly, I think, for he does not know his mind two hours.
I'm sure I left him just now in a humor to be mad, and I 655
think I have not found him very quiet at this present.
(*One knocks.*)   Who's there?

VALENTINE.

>Go see, you sot. —I'm very glad that I can move your
mirth, though not your compassion.   *Exit* Jeremy.

ANGELICA.

>I did not think you had apprehension enough to be 660
exceptious. But madmen show themselves most by ever pre-
tending to a sound understanding, as drunken men do by
over-acting sobriety. I was half inclining to believe you,
till I accidentally touched upon your tender part. But now
you have restored me to my former opinion and compassion. 665

Enter Jeremy.

JEREMY.

>Sir, your father has sent to know if you are any better yet.
Will you please to be mad, sir, or how?

VALENTINE.

>Stupidity! You know the penalty of all I'm worth must pay
for the confession of my senses; I'm mad, and will be mad to
everybody but this lady.   670

JEREMY.

>So—just the very backside of Truth. But lying is a figure in
speech that interlards the greatest part of my conversation.
Madam, your ladyship's woman.   *Goes to the door* [*and leaves*].

Enter Jenny.

ANGELICA.

>Well, have you been there? Come hither.

JENNY.

>Yes, madam.   (*Aside to* Angelica.)   Sir Sampson will wait 675
upon you presently.

VALENTINE.

>You are not leaving me in this uncertainty?

673.1.] SCENE XX *WI.*

---

661. *exceptious*] peevish, captious.

ANGELICA.

Would anything but a madman complain of uncertainty?
Uncertainty and expectation are the joys of life. Security is
an insipid thing, and the overtaking and possessing of a wish 680
discovers the folly of the chase. Never let us know one
another better, for the pleasure of a masquerade is done
when we come to show faces. But I'll tell you two things
before I leave you: I am not the fool you take me for, and
you are mad and don't know it. 685

Exeunt Angelica *and* Jenny.

VALENTINE.

From a riddle you can expect nothing but a riddle. There's
my instruction, and the moral of my lesson.

Re-enter Jeremy.

JEREMY.

What, is the lady gone again, sir? I hope you understood
one another before she went?

VALENTINE.

Understood! She is harder to be understood than a piece of 690
Egyptian antiquity or an Irish manuscript. You may pore
till you spoil your eyes, and not improve your knowledge.

JEREMY.

I have heard 'em say, sir, they read hard Hebrew books
backwards. Maybe you begin to read at the wrong end.

VALENTINE.

They say so of a witch's prayer, and dreams and Dutch 695
almanacs are to be understood by contraries. But there's
regularity and method in that. She is a medal without a
reverse or inscription, for indifference has both sides alike.
Yet while she does not seem to hate me, I will pursue her,
and know her if it be possible, in spite of the opinion of my 700
satirical friend, Scandal, who says,

That women are like tricks by slight of hand,
Which, to admire, we should not understand. *Exeunt.*

The End of the Fourth Act

686.] SCENE XXI *W1.*

ACT V

A room in Foresight's house.
Enter Angelica *and* Jenny.

ANGELICA.

Where is Sir Sampson? Did you not tell me he would be
here before me?

JENNY.

He's at the great glass in the dining room, madam, setting
his cravat and wig.

ANGELICA.

How! I'm glad on't. If he has a mind I should like him, it's   5
a sign he likes me, and that's more than half my design.

JENNY.

I hear him, madam.

ANGELICA.

Leave me, and, d'ye hear, if Valentine should come, or send,
I am not to be spoken with.   *Exit* Jenny.

Enter Sir Sampson.

SIR SAMPSON.

I have not been honored with the commands of a fair lady   10
a great while. Odd, madam, you have revived me—not
since I was five and thirty.

ANGELICA.

Why, you have no great reason to complain, Sir Sampson;
that is not long ago.

SIR SAMPSON.

Zooks, but it is, madam, a very great while, to a man that   15
admires a fine woman as much as I do.

ANGELICA.

You're an absolute courtier, Sir Sampson.

SIR SAMPSON.

Not at all, madam; odsbud, you wrong me; I am not so old
neither to be a bare courtier, only a man of words. Odd, I
have warm blood about me yet; I can serve a lady anyway.   20
Come, come, let me tell you, you women think a man old

9.1.] SCENE II *WI.*

---

too soon, faith and troth you do. Come, don't despise fifty;
odd, fifty, in a hale constitution, is no such contemptible age.

ANGELICA.

Fifty a contemptible age! Not at all, a very fashionable age,
I think. I assure you I know very considerable beaux that   25
set a good face upon fifty. Fifty! I have seen fifty in a side
box, by candlelight, out-blossom five and twenty.

SIR SAMPSON.

O pox, outsides, outsides; a pize take 'em, mere outsides.
Hang your side-box beaux; no, I'm none of those, none of
your forced trees, that pretend to blossom in the fall, and   30
bud when they should bring forth fruit. I am of a long-lived
race, and inherit vigor; none of my family married till fifty,
yet they begot sons and daughters till fourscore. I am of
your patriarchs, I, a branch of one of your antediluvian
families, fellows that the flood could not wash away. Well,   35
madam, what are your commands? Has any young rogue
affronted you, and shall I cut his throat? or—

ANGELICA.

No, Sir Sampson, I have no quarrel upon my hands; I have
more occasion for your conduct than your courage at this
time. To tell you the truth, I'm weary of living single, and   40
want a husband.

SIR SAMPSON (*aside*).

Odsbud, and 'tis pity you should; odd, would she would
like me; then I should hamper my young rogues. Odd,
would she would; faith and troth, she's devilish handsome.
—Madam, you deserve a good husband, and 'twere pity   45
you should be thrown away upon any of these young idle
rogues about the town. Odd, there's ne'er a young fellow
worth hanging—that's a very young fellow. Pize on 'em,
they never think beforehand of anything, and if they commit
matrimony, 'tis as they commit murder, out of a frolic. And   50
are ready to hang themselves, or to be hanged by the law,
the next morning. Odso, have a care madam.

ANGELICA.

Therefore I ask your advice, Sir Sampson. I have fortune
enough to make any man easy that I can like. If there were

26–27. *a side box*] the part of a theater frequented by the beaux and wits.

such a thing as a young, agreeable man, with a reasonable   55
stock of good nature and sense—for I would neither have an
absolute wit, nor a fool.

SIR SAMPSON.

Odd, you are hard to please, madam; to find a young fellow
that is neither a wit in his own eye, nor a fool in the eye of
the world, is a very hard task. But, faith and troth, you   60
speak very discreetly, for I hate both a wit and a fool.

ANGELICA.

She that marries a fool, Sir Sampson, commits the reputation of her honesty or understanding to the censure of the
world. And she that marries a very witty man submits both
to the severity and insolent conduct of her husband. I should   65
like a man of wit for a lover, because I would have such a
one in my power, but I would no more be his wife than his
enemy. For his malice is not a more terrible consequence of
his aversion than his jealousy is of his love.

SIR SAMPSON.

None of old Foresight's sibyls ever uttered such a truth.   70
Odsbud, you have won my heart; I hate a wit; I had a son
that was spoiled among 'em, a good, hopeful lad, till he
learned to be a wit, and might have risen in the state. But, a
pox on't, his wit run him out of his money, and now his
poverty has run him out of his wits.   75

ANGELICA.

Sir Sampson, as your friend, I must tell you, you are very
much abused in that matter. He's no more mad than you
are.

SIR SAMPSON.

How, madam! Would I could prove it.

ANGELICA.

I can tell you how that may be done. But it is a thing that   80
would make me appear to be too much concerned in your
affairs.

SIR SAMPSON (*aside*).

Odsbud, I believe she likes me. —Ah, madam, all my
affairs are scarce worthy to be laid at your feet. And I wish,
madam, they stood in a better posture, that I might make a   85
more becoming offer to a lady of your incomparable beauty
and merit. If I had Peru in one hand and Mexico in t'other,

and the Eastern Empire under my feet, it would make me
only a more glorious victim to be offered at the shrine of
your beauty.   90

ANGELICA.

Bless me, Sir Sampson, what's the matter?

SIR SAMPSON.

Odd, madam, I love you, and if you would take my advice
in a husband—

ANGELICA.

Hold, hold, Sir Sampson. I asked your advice for a husband,
and you are giving me your consent. I was indeed thinking   95
to propose something like it in a jest, to satisfy you about
Valentine, for if a match were seemingly carried on between
you and me, it would oblige him to throw off his disguise of
madness in apprehension of losing me, for you know he has
long pretended a passion for me.   100

SIR SAMPSON.

Gadzooks, a most ingenious contrivance—if we were to go
through with it. But why must the match only be seemingly
carried on? Odd, let it be a real contract.

ANGELICA.

O fie, Sir Sampson, what would the world say?

SIR SAMPSON.

Say, they would say, you were a wise woman, and I a happy   105
man. Odd, madam, I'll love you as long as I live, and leave
you a good jointure when I die.

ANGELICA.

Aye, but that is not in your power, Sir Sampson, for when
Valentine confesses himself in his senses, he must make over
his inheritance to his younger brother.   110

SIR SAMPSON.

Odd, you're cunning, a wary baggage! Faith and troth, I
like you the better. But, I warrant you, I have a proviso in
the obligation in favor of myself. Body o'me, I have a trick
to turn the settlement upon the issue male of our two bodies
begotten. Odsbud, let us find children, and I'll find an estate.   115

ANGELICA.

Will you? Well, do you find the estate, and leave t'other to
me—

96. in a jest] *Q1–3*; in jest *Q4, W1.*

SIR SAMPSON.

O rogue! But I'll trust you. And will you consent? Is it a
match then?

ANGELICA.

Let me consult my lawyer concerning this obligation, and 120
if I find what you propose practicable, I'll give you my
answer.

SIR SAMPSON.

With all my heart. Come in with me, and I'll lend you the
bond. You shall consult your lawyer, and I'll consult a
parson. Odzooks, I'm a young man; odzooks, I'm a young 125
man, and I'll make it appear— Odd, you're devilish handsome; faith and troth, you're very handsome, and I'm very
young, and very lusty. Odsbud, hussy, you know how to
choose, and so do I. Odd, I think we are very well met.
Give me your hand; odd, let me kiss it; 'tis as warm and as 130
soft—as what?—odd, as t'other hand—and give me t'other
hand, and I'll mumble 'em, and kiss 'em till they melt in
my mouth.

ANGELICA.

Hold, Sir Sampson, you're profuse of your vigor before
your time; you'll spend your estate before you come to it. 135

SIR SAMPSON.

No, no, only give me a rent-roll of my possessions. Ah!
baggage, I warrant you, for little Sampson. Odd, Sampson's
a very good name for an able fellow; your Sampsons were
strong dogs from the beginning.

ANGELICA.

Have a care, and don't overact your part. If you remember, 140
the strongest Sampson of your name pulled an old house
over his head at last.

SIR SAMPSON.

Say you so, hussy? Come let's go then. Odd, I long to be
pulling down too, come away. Odso, here's somebody
coming.   *Exeunt.* 145

Enter Tattle *and* Jeremy.

TATTLE.

Is not that she, gone out just now?

145.1.] SCENE III *W1.*

---

136. *rent-roll*] inventory or schedule of properties.

JEREMY.

>Aye, sir, she's just going to the place of appointment. Ah,
>sir, if you are not very faithful and close in this business,
>you'll certainly be the death of a person that has a most
>extraordinary passion for your honor's service.   150

TATTLE.

>Aye, who's that?

JEREMY.

>Even my unworthy self, sir. Sir, I have had an appetite to be
>fed with your commands a great while. And now, sir, my
>former master having much troubled the fountain of his
>understanding, it is a very plausible occasion for me to   155
>quench my thirst at the spring of your bounty. I thought I
>could not recommend myself better to you, sir, than by the
>delivery of a great beauty and fortune into your arms,
>whom I have heard you sigh for.

TATTLE.

>I'll make thy fortune; say no more. Thou art a pretty fellow,   160
>and canst carry a message to a lady in a pretty soft kind of
>phrase, and with a good persuading accent.

JEREMY.

>Sir, I have the seeds of rhetoric and oratory in my head.
>I have been at Cambridge.

TATTLE.

>Aye, 'tis well enough for a servant to be bred at an university,   165
>but the education is a little too pedantic for a gentleman.
>I hope you are secret in your nature, private, close, ha?

JEREMY.

>O sir, for that, sir, 'tis my chief talent; I'm as secret as the
>head of Nilus.

TATTLE.

>Aye? Who's he, though? a privy counselor?   170

JEREMY (*aside*).

>O ignorance!—A cunning Egyptian, sir, that with his arms
>would overrun the country, yet nobody could ever find out
>his headquarters.

TATTLE.

>Close dog! A good whoremaster, I warrant him. The time

162. phrase] *Q1–Q3, W1*; praise *Q4.*

draws nigh, Jeremy. Angelica will be veiled like a nun, and 175
I must be hooded like a friar, ha, Jeremy?

JEREMY.

Aye, sir, hooded like a hawk, to seize at first sight upon the
quarry. It is the whim of my master's madness to be so
dressed, and she is so in love with him, she'll comply with
anything to please him. Poor lady, I'm sure she'll have 180
reason to pray for me when she finds what a happy exchange
she has made, between a madman and so accomplished a
gentleman.

TATTLE.

Aye, faith, so she will, Jeremy; you're a good friend to her,
poor creature. I swear I do it hardly so much in considera- 185
tion of myself as compassion to her.

JEREMY.

'Tis an act of charity, sir, to save a fine woman with thirty
thousand pound from throwing herself away.

TATTLE.

So 'tis, faith. I might have saved several others in my time,
but I, gad, I could never find in my heart to marry anybody 190
before.

JEREMY.

Well, sir, I'll go and tell her my master's coming, and meet
you in half a quarter of an hour, with your disguise, at your
own lodgings. You must talk a little madly; she won't
distinguish the tone of your voice.   195

TATTLE.

No, no, let me alone for a counterfeit; I'll be ready for you.

Enter Miss Prue.

MISS PRUE.

O, Mr. Tattle, are you here! I'm glad I have found you; I
have been looking up and down for you like anything, till
I'm as tired as anything in the world.

TATTLE (*aside*).

O pox, how shall I get rid of this foolish girl?   200

MISS PRUE.

O, I have pure news; I can tell you pure news. I must not

196.1.] SCENE IV *W1.*

marry the seaman now; my father says so. Why won't you
be my husband? You say you love me, and you won't be my
husband. And I know you may be my husband now if you
please.   205

TATTLE.

O fie, miss, who told you so, child?

MISS PRUE.

Why, my father. I told him that you loved me.

TATTLE.

O fie, miss, why did you do so? And who told you so, child?

MISS PRUE.

Who? Why, you did, did not you?

TATTLE.

O pox, that was yesterday, miss; that was a great while ago, 210
child. I have been asleep since, slept a whole night, and did
not so much as dream of the matter.

MISS PRUE.

Pshaw, O, but I dreamt that it was so, though.

TATTLE.

Aye, but your father will tell you that dreams come by
contraries, child. O fie; what, we must not love one another 215
now; phsaw, that would be a foolish thing indeed. Fie, fie,
you're a woman now, and must think of a new man every
morning, and forget him every night. No, no, to marry is to
be a child again and play with the same rattle always; O
fie, marrying is a paw thing.   220

MISS PRUE.

Well, but don't you love me as well as you did last night,
then?

TATTLE.

No, no, child, you would not have me.

MISS PRUE.

No? Yes, but I would, though.

TATTLE.

Pshaw, but I tell you, you would not. You forget you're a 225
woman, and don't know your own mind.

MISS PRUE.

But here's my father, and he knows my mind.

---

220. *paw*] silly, stupid.

Enter Foresight.

FORESIGHT.

O, Mr. Tattle, your servant; you are a close man, but
methinks your love to my daughter was a secret I might
have been trusted with. Or had you a mind to try if I could   230
discover it by my art. Hum, ha! I think there is something
in your physiognomy that has a resemblance of her, and the
girl is like me.

TATTLE.

And so you would infer that you and I are alike.   (*Aside.*)
What does the old prig mean? I'll banter him, and laugh at   235
him, and leave him. —I fancy you have a wrong notion of
faces.

FORESIGHT.

How? What? A wrong notion? How so?

TATTLE.

In the way of art. I have some taking features, not obvious
to vulgar eyes, that are indications of a sudden turn of good   240
fortune in the lottery of wives, and promise of great beauty
and great fortune reserved alone for me, by a private intrigue
of destiny, kept secret from the piercing eye of perspicuity,
from all astrologers and the stars themselves.

FORESIGHT.

How! I will make it appear that what you say is impossible.   245

TATTLE.

Sir, I beg your pardon; I'm in haste—

FORESIGHT.

For what?

TATTLE.

To be married, sir, married.

FORESIGHT.

Aye, but pray take me along with you, sir—

TATTLE.

No, sir; 'tis to be done privately. I never make confidants.   250

FORESIGHT.

Well, but my consent, I mean. You won't marry my
daughter without my consent?

227.1.] SCENE V *W1.*

-123-

TATTLE.

Who, I, sir? I'm an absolute stranger to you and your
daughter, sir.

FORESIGHT.

Hey day! What time of the moon is this?   255

TATTLE.

Very true, sir, and desire to continue so. I have no more love
for your daughter than I have likeness of you, and I have a
secret in my heart, which you would be glad to know, and
shan't know, and yet you shall know it too, and be sorry for't
afterwards. I'd have you to know, sir, that I am as knowing 260
as the stars, and as secret as the night. And I'm going to be
married just now, yet did not know of it half an hour ago,
and the lady stays for me, and does not know of it yet.
There's a mystery for you; I know you love to untie
difficulties. Or if you can't solve this, stay here a quarter of 265
an hour, and I'll come and explain it to you.   *Exit.*

MISS PRUE.

O Father, why will you let him go? Won't you make him
be my husband?

FORESIGHT.

Mercy on us, what do these lunacies portend? Alas, he's
mad, child, stark wild.   270

MISS PRUE.

What, and must not I have e'er a husband then? What,
must I go to bed to Nurse again, and be a child as long as
she's an old woman? Indeed, but I won't; for now my mind
is set upon a man, I will have a man some way or other. O!
methinks I'm sick when I think of a man, and if I can't have 275
one, I would go to sleep all my life, for when I'm awake, it
makes me wish and long, and I don't know for what—and
I'd rather be always sleeping, than sick with thinking.

FORESIGHT.

O fearful! I think the girl's influenced too. Hussy, you shall
have a rod.   280

MISS PRUE.

A fiddle of a rod, I'll have a husband, and if you won't get

267.] SCENE VI *W1.*

---

255. *What . . . this?*] What is the astrological situation?

me one, I'll get one for myself; I'll marry our Robin, the
butler. He says he loves me, and he's a handsome man, and
shall be my husband; I warrant he'll be my husband and
thank me too, for he told me so.   285

Enter Scandal, Mrs. Foresight, *and* Nurse.

FORESIGHT.

Did he so—I'll dispatch him for't presently. Rogue!—O,
Nurse, come hither.

NURSE.

What is your worship's pleasure?

FORESIGHT.

Here, take your young mistress, and lock her up presently,
till farther orders from me. Not a word, hussy; do what I   290
bid you, no reply, away. And bid Robin make ready to
give an account of his plate and linen; d'ee hear, be gone
when I bid you.   *Exeunt* Nurse *and* Miss Prue.

MRS. FORESIGHT.

What's the matter, husband?

FORESIGHT.

'Tis not convenient to tell you now. —Mr. Scandal, heaven 295
keep us all in our senses; I fear there is a contagious frenzy
abroad. How does Valentine?

SCANDAL.

O, I hope he will do well again. I have a message from him
to your niece Angelica.

FORESIGHT.

I think she has not returned since she went abroad with Sir 300
Sampson.

Enter Ben.

MRS. FORESIGHT.

Here's Mr. Benjamin, he can tell us if his father be come
home.

BEN.

Who, father? aye, he's come home with a vengeance.

285.1.] SCENE VII *W1*.   why are you not gone?
293. S.D.] *W1 omits.*   301.1.] SCENE VIII *W1*.
301. Sampson] *W1 adds*: Nurse,

MRS. FORESIGHT.

> Why, what's the matter?   305

BEN.

> Matter! Why, he's mad.

FORESIGHT.

> Mercy on us, I was afraid of this.

BEN.

> And there's the handsome young woman, she, as they say,
> brother Val went mad for; she's mad too, I think.

FORESIGHT.

> O my poor niece, my poor niece, is she gone too? Well, I 310
> shall run mad next.

MRS. FORESIGHT.

> Well, but how mad? How d'ee mean?

BEN.

> Nay, I'll give you leave to guess. I'll undertake to make a
> voyage to Antegoa. No, hold, I mayn't say so neither, but
> I'll sail as far as Leghorn, and back again, before you shall 315
> guess at the matter, and do nothing else. Mess, you may
> take in all the points of the compass, and not hit right.

MRS. FORESIGHT.

> Your experiment will take up a little too much time.

BEN.

> Why, then, I'll tell you, there's a new wedding upon the
> stocks, and they two are a-going to be married to rights.   320

SCANDAL.

> Who?

BEN.

> Why, father and—the young woman. I can't hit of her
> name.

SCANDAL.

> Angelica?

BEN.

> Aye, the same.   325

MRS. FORESIGHT.

> Sir Sampson and Angelica, impossible!

---

314. *Antegoa*] Antigua, a colony of the West Indies.
315. *Leghorn*] a port in northwest Italy.

BEN.

That may be, but I'm sure it is as I tell you.

SCANDAL.

'Sdeath, it's a jest. I can't believe it.

BEN.

Look you, friend, it's nothing to me whether you believe it
or no. What I say is true; d'ee see, they are married, or just 330
going to be married, I know not which.

FORESIGHT.

Well, but they are not mad, that is, not lunatic?

BEN.

I don't know what you may call madness, but she's mad
for a husband, and he's horn-mad, I think, or they'd ne'er
make a match together. —Here they come.   335

Enter Sir Sampson, Angelica, *with* Buckram.

SIR SAMPSON.

Where is this old soothsayer? this uncle of mine elect?
Aha, old Foresight, Uncle Foresight, wish me joy, Uncle
Foresight, double joy, both as uncle and astrologer. Here's
a conjunction that was not foretold in all your Ephemeris.
The brightest star in the blue firmament—is shot from 340
above, in a jelly of love, and so forth, and I'm lord of the
ascendant. Odd, you're an old fellow, Foresight; Uncle I
mean, a very old fellow, Uncle Foresight, and yet you shall
live to dance at my wedding; faith and troth, you shall.
Odd, we'll have the music of the spheres for thee, old Lilly, 345
that we will, and thou shalt lead up a dance in *via lactea*.

FORESIGHT.

I'm thunderstruck! You are not married to my niece?

SIR SAMPSON.

Not absolutely married, Uncle, but very near it, within a
kiss of the matter, as you see.   *Kisses* Angelica.

ANGELICA.

'Tis very true indeed, Uncle; I hope you'll be my father, 350
and give me.

335.1.] SCENE IX *W1*.

---

334. *horn-mad*] so deranged as to be dangerous.
346. *via lactea*] the Milky Way.

SIR SAMPSON.

That he shall, or I'll burn his globes. Body o'me, he shall be
thy father, I'll make him thy father, and thou shalt make me
a father, and I'll make thee a mother, and we'll beget sons
and daughters enough to put the weekly bills out of 355
countenance.

SCANDAL.

Death and hell! Where's Valentine?   *Exit* Scandal.

MRS. FORESIGHT.

This is so surprising—

SIR SAMPSON.

How! What does my aunt say? Surprising, aunt? Not at all,
for a young couple to make a match in winter? Not at all— 360
it's a plot to undermine cold weather, and destroy that
usurper of a bed called a warming pan.

MRS. FORESIGHT.

I'm glad to hear you have so much fire in you, Sir Sampson.

BEN.

Mess, I fear his fire's little better than tinder; mayhap it
will only serve to light up a match for somebody else. The 365
young woman's a handsome young woman, I can't deny it,
but, father, if I might be your pilot in this case, you should
not marry her. It's just the same thing as if so be you should
sail so far as the Straits without provision.

SIR SAMPSON.

Who gave you the authority to speak, sirrah? To your 370
element, fish, be mute, fish, and to sea; rule your helm,
sirrah, don't direct me.

BEN.

Well, well, take you care of your own helm, or you mayn't
keep your own vessel steady.

SIR SAMPSON.

Why, you impudent tarpaulin! Sirrah, do you bring your 375
forecastle jests upon your father? But I shall be even with
you; I won't give you a groat. Mr. Buckram, is the conveyance so worded that nothing can possibly descend to this
scoundrel? I would not so much as have him have the

358.] SCENE X *WI*.   374. own] *Q1–3*; new *Q4, WI.*

___

369. *Straits*] the passage through the Bosporus and Dardanelles.

prospect of an estate, though there were no way to come 380
to it, but by the Northeast Passage.

BUCKRAM.

Sir, it is drawn according to your directions; there is not the
least cranny of the law unstopt.

BEN.

Lawyer, I believe there's many a cranny and leak unstopt
in your conscience. If so be that one had a pump in your 385
bosom, I believe we should discover a foul hold. They say a
witch will sail in a sieve, but I believe the devil would not
venture aboard o'your conscience. And that's for you.

SIR SAMPSON.

Hold your tongue, sirrah. How now, who's there?

Enter Tattle *and* Mrs. Frail.

MRS. FRAIL.

O, sister, the most unlucky accident! 390

MRS. FORESIGHT.

What's the matter?

TATTLE.

O, the two most unfortunate poor creatures in the world we
are.

FORESIGHT.

Bless us! How so?

MRS. FRAIL.

Ah, Mr. Tattle and I, poor Mr. Tattle and I are—I can't 395
speak it out.

TATTLE.

Nor I—but poor Mrs. Frail and I are—

MRS. FRAIL.

Married.

MRS. FORESIGHT.

Married! How?

TATTLE.

Suddenly—before we knew where we were—that villain 400
Jeremy, by the help of disguises, tricked us into one another.

FORESIGHT.

Why, you told me just now you went hence in haste to be
married.

389.1.] SCENE XI *W1*.

—129—

ANGELICA.

But I believe Mr. Tattle meant the favor to me. I thank him.

TATTLE.

I did; as I hope to be saved, madam, my intentions were 405
good. But this is the most cruel thing, to marry one does not
know how, nor why, nor wherefore. The devil take me if
ever I was so much concerned at anything in my life.

ANGELICA.

'Tis very unhappy, if you don't care for one another.

TATTLE.

The least in the world—that is for my part; I speak for 410
myself. Gad, I never had the least thought of serious kindness; I never liked anybody less in my life. Poor woman!
Gad, I'm sorry for her too, for I have no reason to hate her
neither, but I believe I shall lead her a damned sort of a life.

MRS. FORESIGHT [aside to Mrs. Frail].

He's better than no husband at all, though he's a coxcomb. 415

MRS. FRAIL (to her).

Aye, aye, it's well it's no worse. —Nay, for my part I always
despised Mr. Tattle of all things; nothing but his being my
husband could have made me like him less.

TATTLE.

Look you there, I thought as much. Pox on't, I wish we
could keep it secret. Why, I don't believe any of this 420
company would speak of it.

MRS. FRAIL.

But, my dear, that's impossible; the parson and that rogue
Jeremy will publish it.

TATTLE.

Aye, my dear, so they will, as you say.

ANGELICA.

O, you'll agree very well in a little time; custom will make 425
it easy for you.

TATTLE.

Easy! Pox on't, I don't believe I shall sleep tonight.

SIR SAMPSON.

Sleep, quotha! No, why you would not sleep o'your wedding
night? I'm an older fellow than you, and don't mean to
sleep.   430

BEN.

> Why, there's another match now, as thof a couple of priva-
> teers were looking for a prize and should fall foul of one
> another. I'm sorry for the young man with all my heart. Look
> you, friend, if I may advise you, when she's going, for that
> you must expect, I have experience of her; when she's going, 435
> let her go. For no matrimony is tough enough to hold her, and
> if she can't drag her anchor along with her, she'll break her
> cable. I can tell you that. Who's here? The madman?

Enter Valentine *dressed*, Scandal, *and* Jeremy.

VALENTINE.

> No, here's the fool, and if occasion be, I'll give it under my
> hand.   440

SIR SAMPSON.

> How now?

VALENTINE.

> Sir, I'm come to acknowledge my errors, and ask your
> pardon.

SIR SAMPSON.

> What, have you found your senses at last then? In good
> time, sir.   445

VALENTINE.

> You were abused, sir; I never was distracted.

FORESIGHT.

> How! Not mad! Mr. Scandal.

SCANDAL.

> No really, sir; I'm his witness; it was all counterfeit.

VALENTINE.

> I thought I had reasons. But it was a poor contrivance; the
> effect has shown it such.   450

SIR SAMPSON.

> Contrivance, what, to cheat me? To cheat your father,
> sirrah, could you hope to prosper?

VALENTINE.

> Indeed, I thought, sir, when the father endeavored to undo
> the son, it was a reasonable return of nature.

438.1.] SCENE *The Last W1.*

439–440. *give . . . hand*] acknowledge it, possibly under oath.

SIR SAMPSON.

> Very good, sir. Mr. Buckram, are you ready? Come, sir, will 455
> you sign and seal?

VALENTINE.

> If you please, sir; but first I would ask this lady one question.

SIR SAMPSON.

> Sir, you must ask my leave first. That lady, no, sir; you shall
> ask that lady no questions, till you have asked her blessing,
> sir; that lady is to be my wife. 460

VALENTINE.

> I have heard as much, sir, but I would have it from her own
> mouth.

SIR SAMPSON.

> That's as much as to say I lie, sir, and you don't believe
> what I say.

VALENTINE.

> Pardon me, sir. But I reflect that I very lately counterfeited 465
> madness; I don't know but the frolic may go round.

SIR SAMPSON.

> Come, chuck, satisfy him, answer him. Come, come, Mr.
> Buckram, the pen and ink.

BUCKRAM.

> Here it is, sir, with the deed; all is ready.

> > *Valentine goes to* Angelica.

ANGELICA.

> 'Tis true, you have a great while pretended love to me; nay, 470
> what if you were sincere? Still you must pardon me, if I
> think my own inclinations have a better right to dispose of
> my person, than yours.

SIR SAMPSON.

> Are you answered now, sir?

VALENTINE.

> Yes, sir. 475

SIR SAMPSON.

> Where's your plot, sir, and your contrivance now, sir?
> Will you sign, sir? Come, will you sign and seal?

VALENTINE.

> With all my heart, sir.

458. my] *Q1–3*; me *Q4, W1*.

SCANDAL.

    'Sdeath, you are not mad, indeed, to ruin yourself?

VALENTINE.

    I have been disappointed of my only hope, and he that 480
loses hope may part with anything. I never valued fortune,
but as it was subservient to my pleasure, and my only
pleasure was to please this lady. I have made many vain
attempts, and find, at last, nothing but my ruin can effect it.
    Which for that reason, I will sign to—give me the paper.   485

ANGELICA (*aside*).

    Generous Valentine!

BUCKRAM.

    Here is the deed, sir.

VALENTINE.

    But where is the bond by which I am obliged to sign this?

BUCKRAM.

    Sir Sampson, you have it.

ANGELICA.

    No, I have it, and I'll use it as I would everything that is 490
enemy to Valentine.   *Tears the paper.*

SIR SAMPSON.

    How now!

VALENTINE.

    Ha!

ANGELICA.

    Had I the world to give you, it could not make me worthy of
so generous and faithful a passion. (*To* Valentine.) 495
Here's my hand, my heart was always yours, and struggled
very hard to make this utmost trial of your virtue.

VALENTINE.

    Between pleasure and amazement, I am lost—but on my
knees I take the blessing.

SIR SAMPSON.

    Oons, what is the meaning of this?   500

BEN.

    Mess, here's the wind changed again. Father, you and I
may make a voyage together now.

ANGELICA.

    Well, Sir Sampson, since I have played you a trick, I'll advise
you how you may avoid such another. Learn to be a good

father, or you'll never get a second wife. I always loved 505
your son, and hated your unforgiving nature. I was resolved
to try him to the utmost; I have tried you too, and know you
both. You have not more faults than he has virtues, and 'tis
hardly more pleasure to me that I can make him and
myself happy, than that I can punish you.   510

VALENTINE.

If my happiness could receive addition, this kind surprise
would make it double.

SIR SAMPSON.

Oons, you're a crocodile.

FORESIGHT.

Really, Sir Sampson, this is a sudden eclipse—

SIR SAMPSON.

You're an illiterate fool, and I'm another, and the stars are 515
liars, and if I had breath enough, I'd curse them and you,
myself, and everybody. Oons, cullied, bubbled, jilted,
woman-bobbed at last; I have not patience. *Exit* Sir Sampson.

TATTLE.

If the gentleman is in this disorder for want of a wife, I can
spare him mine. O, are you there, sir? (*To* Jeremy.) I'm 520
indebted to you for my happiness.

JEREMY.

Sir, I ask you ten thousand pardons, 'twas an errant
mistake. You see, sir, my master was never mad, nor
anything like it. Then how could it be otherwise?

VALENTINE.

Tattle, I thank you, you would have interposed between me 525
and heaven, but Providence laid purgatory in your way.
You have but justice.

SCANDAL.

I hear the fiddles that Sir Sampson provided for his own
wedding; methinks 'tis pity they should not be employed
when the match is so much mended. Valentine, though it 530
be morning, we may have a dance.

VALENTINE.

Anything, my friend, everything that looks like joy and
transport.

SCANDAL.

Call 'em, Jeremy.

ANGELICA.

    I have done dissembling now, Valentine, and if that cold- 535
ness which I have always worn before you should turn to an
extreme fondness, you must not suspect it.

VALENTINE.

    I'll prevent that suspicion, for I intend to dote on at that
immoderate rate that your fondness shall never distinguish
itself enough to be taken notice of. If ever you seem to love 540
too much, it must be only when I can't love enough.

ANGELICA.

    Have a care of large promises; you know you are apt to run
more in debt than you are able to pay.

VALENTINE.

    Therefore I yield my body as your prisoner, and make your
best on't.   545

SCANDAL.

    The music stays for you.

Dance.

    Well, madam, you have done exemplary justice in punishing
an inhuman father, and rewarding a faithful lover. But there
is a third good work which I, in particular, must thank you
for; I was an infidel to your sex, and you have converted me. 550
For now I am convinced that all women are not like fortune,
blind in bestowing favors, either on those who do not merit,
or who do not want 'em.

ANGELICA.

    'Tis an unreasonable accusation that you lay upon our sex.
You tax us with injustice, only to cover your own want of 555
merit. You would all have the reward of love, but few have
the constancy to stay till it becomes your due. Men are
generally hypocrites and infidels; they pretend to worship,
but have neither zeal nor faith. How few, like Valentine,
would persevere even unto martyrdom, and sacrifice their 560
interest to their constancy! In admiring me, you misplace
the novelty.

          The miracle today is that we find
          A lover true: not that a woman's kind.

                          Exeunt Omnes.

FINIS

542. large] *Q4 and W1 omit.*

Appendix

Chronology

Approximate years are indicated by *.

Political and Literary Events	Life and Major Works of Congreve

1631
Death of Donne.
John Dryden born.
Shirley's *THE TRAITOR*.

1633
Samuel Pepys born.

1635
Sir George Etherege born.*

1640
Aphra Behn born.*

1641
William Wycherley born.*

1642
First Civil War began (ended 1646).
Theaters closed by Parliament.
Thomas Shadwell born.*

1648
Second Civil War.

1649
Execution of Charles I.

1650
Jeremy Collier born.

1651
Hobbes' *Leviathan* published.

1652
First Dutch War began (ended 1654).
Thomas Otway born.

1653
Nathaniel Lee born.*

1656
D'Avenant's *THE SIEGE OF RHODES* performed at Rutland House.

1657
John Dennis born.

1658
Death of Oliver Cromwell.
D'Avenant's *THE CRUELTY OF THE SPANIARDS IN PERU* performed at the Cockpit.

1660
Restoration of Charles II.
Theatrical patents granted to Thomas Killigrew and Sir William D'Avenant, authorizing them to form, respectively, the King's and the Duke of York's Companies.
Pepys began his diary.

1661
Cowley's *THE CUTTER OF COLEMAN STREET.*
D'Avenant's *THE SIEGE OF RHODES* (expanded to two parts).

1662
Charter granted to the Royal Society.

1663
Dryden's *THE WILD GALLANT.*
Tuke's *THE ADVENTURES OF FIVE HOURS.*

1664
Sir John Vanbrugh born.
Dryden's *THE RIVAL LADIES.*
Dryden and Howard's *THE INDIAN QUEEN.*
Etherege's *THE COMICAL REVENGE.*

1665
Second Dutch War began (ended 1667).
Great Plague.
Dryden's *THE INDIAN EM-PEROR*.
Orrery's *MUSTAPHA*.

1666
Fire of London.
Death of James Shirley.

1667
Jonathan Swift born.
Milton's *Paradise Lost* published.
Sprat's *The History of the Royal Society* published.
Dryden's *SECRET LOVE*.

1668
Death of D'Avenant.
Dryden made Poet Laureate.
Dryden's *An Essay of Dramatic Poesy* published.
Shadwell's *THE SULLEN LOVERS*.

1669
Pepys terminated his diary.
Susannah Centlivre born.

1670
Dryden's *THE CONQUEST OF GRANADA*, Part I.

Born on January 24 at Bardsey, near Leeds, Yorkshire.

1671
Dorset Garden Theatre (Duke's Company) opened.
Colley Cibber born.
Milton's *Paradise Regained* and *Samson Agonistes* published.
Dryden's *THE CONQUEST OF GRANADA*, Part II.
THE REHEARSAL, by the Duke of Buckingham and others.
Wycherley's *LOVE IN A WOOD*.

1672
Third Dutch War began (ended 1674).

Joseph Addison born.
Richard Steele born.
Dryden's *MARRIAGE À LA MODE.*

1674
New Drury Lane Theatre (King's Company) opened.
Death of Milton.
Nicholas Rowe born.
Thomas Rymer's *Reflections on Aristotle's Treatise of Poesy* (translation of Rapin) published.

Lived at Youghal and Carrickfergus in Ireland (1674–1681).

1675
Dryden's *AURENG-ZEBE.*
Wycherley's *THE COUNTRY WIFE.* *

1676
Etherege's *THE MAN OF MODE.*
Otway's *DON CARLOS.*
Shadwell's *THE VIRTUOSO.*
Wycherley's *THE PLAIN DEALER.*

1677
Rymer's *Tragedies of the Last Age Considered* published.
Aphra Behn's *THE ROVER.*
Dryden's *ALL FOR LOVE*
Lee's *THE RIVAL QUEENS.*

1678
Popish Plot.
George Farquhar born.
Bunyan's *Pilgrim's Progress* (Part I) published.

1679
Exclusion Bill introduced.
Death of Thomas Hobbes.
Death of Roger Boyle, Earl of Orrery.
Charles Johnson born.

1680
Death of Samuel Butler.
Death of John Wilmot, Earl of Rochester.

Dryden's *THE SPANISH FRIAR*.
Lee's *LUCIUS JUNIUS BRUTUS*.
Otway's *THE ORPHAN*.

1681

Charles II dissolved Parliament at
Oxford.
Dryden's *Absalom and Achitophel*
published.
Tate's adaptation of *KING LEAR*.

1682

The King's and the Duke of York's   Entered Kilkenny School, Kilkenny.
Companies merged into the United
Company.
Dryden's *The Medal, MacFlecknoe,*
and *Religio Laici* published.
Otway's *VENICE PRESERVED*.

1683

Rye House Plot.
Death of Thomas Killigrew.
Crowne's *CITY POLITIQUES*.

1685

Death of Charles II; accession of
James II.
Revocation of the Edict of Nantes.
The Duke of Monmouth's Rebellion.
Death of Otway.
John Gay born.
Crowne's *SIR COURTLY NICE*.
Dryden's *ALBION AND AL-
BANIUS*.

1686

On April 5 entered Trinity College,
Dublin.

1687

Death of the Duke of Buckingham.
Dryden's *The Hind and the Panther*
published.
Newton's *Principia* published.

1688

The Revolution.   Returned to England.
Alexander Pope born.

Shadwell's *THE SQUIRE OF ALSATIA.*

1689

The War of the League of Augsburg began (ended 1697).
Toleration Act.
Death of Aphra Behn.
Shadwell made Poet Laureate.
Dryden's *DON SEBASTIAN.*
Shadwell's *BURY FAIR.*

1690

Battle of the Boyne.
Locke's *Two Treatises of Government* and *An Essay concerning Human Understanding* published.

Visited Ireland.

1691

Death of Etherege.*
Langbaine's *An Account of the English Dramatic Poets* published.

Enrolled on March 17 as law student in the Middle Temple, London.

1692

Death of Lee.
Death of Shadwell.
Tate made Poet Laureate.

Published a romance, *Incognita.*
Contributed poems to Charles Gildon's *Miscellany of Original Poems.*
Translated the eleventh satire of Juvenal for Dryden's translation of *The Satires of Juvenal and Persius.*

1693

George Lillo born.*
Rymer's *A Short View of Tragedy* published.

THE OLD BACHELOR produced at Drury Lane on March 9.
THE DOUBLE DEALER produced at Drury Lane in December.

1694

Death of Queen Mary.
Southerne's *THE FATAL MAR-RIAGE.*

Commemorated the death of Queen Mary in *The Mourning Muse of Alexis.*

1695

Group of actors led by Thomas Betterton leave Drury Lane and establish a new company at Lincoln's Inn Fields.
Southerne's *OROONOKO.*

LOVE FOR LOVE produced at Lincoln's Inn Fields on April 30.
Appointed Commissioner of Hackney Coaches.
Published essay *Concerning Humor in Comedy.*

1696
Cibber's *LOVE'S LAST SHIFT*.
Vanbrugh's *THE RELAPSE*.

Visited Ireland and received an honorary M.A. degree from Trinity College in February.

1697
Treaty of Ryswick ended the War of the League of Augsburg.
Charles Macklin born.
Vanbrugh's *THE PROVOKED WIFE*.

THE MOURNING BRIDE produced at Lincoln's Inn Fields, possibly on February 20.

1698
Collier controversy started with the publication of *A Short View of the Immorality and Profaneness of the English Stage*.

Published *Amendments of Mr. Collier's False and Imperfect Citations*.

1699
Farquhar's *THE CONSTANT COUPLE*.

1700
Death of Dryden.
Blackmore's *Satire against Wit* published.

THE WAY OF THE WORLD produced at Lincoln's Inn Fields, probably on March 5.
In late summer and autumn, visited Belgium and Holland with Charles Mein and Jacob Tonson.

1701
Act of Settlement.
War of the Spanish Succession began (ended 1713).
Death of James II.
Rowe's *TAMERLANE*.
Steele's *THE FUNERAL*.

THE JUDGMENT OF PARIS, a masque, produced at Dorset Garden, probably on March 21.

1702
Death of William III; accession of Anne.
The Daily Courant began publication.
Cibber's *SHE WOULD AND SHE WOULD NOT*.

1703
Death of Samuel Pepys.
Rowe's *THE FAIR PENITENT*.

1704

Capture of Gibraltar; Battle of Blenheim.

Defoe's *The Review* began publication (1704–1713).

Swift's *A Tale of a Tub* and *The Battle of the Books* published.

Cibber's *THE CARELESS HUSBAND*.

Collaborated with Vanbrugh and Walsh in *SQUIRE TRELOOBY*, a farce adapted from Molière's *Monsieur de Pourceaugnac* and produced at Lincoln's Inn Fields, probably on March 30.

Joint manager with Vanbrugh of the new Haymarket Theatre, 1704–1705.

1705

Steele's *THE TENDER HUSBAND*.

Published *The Tears of Amaryllis*.

Appointed Commissioner of Wine Licenses.

1706

Battle of Ramillies.

Farquhar's *THE RECRUITING OFFICER*.

1707

Union of Scotland and England.

Death of Farquhar.

Henry Fielding born.

Farquhar's *THE BEAUX' STRATAGEM*.

1708

Downes' *Roscius Anglicanus* published.

1709

Samuel Johnson born.

Rowe's edition of Shakespeare published.

The Tatler began publication (1709–1711).

Centlivre's *THE BUSY BODY*.

1710

Publication of first collected edition of Congreve's works, including *SEMELE*, an opera.

1711

Shaftesbury's *Characteristics* published.

The Spectator began publication (1711–1712).

Pope's *An Essay on Criticism* published.

1713
Treaty of Utrecht ended the War of the Spanish Succession.
Addison's *CATO*.

1714
Death of Anne; accession of George I.
Steele became Governor of Drury Lane.
John Rich assumed management of Lincoln's Inn Fields.
Centlivre's *THE WONDER: A WOMAN KEEPS A SECRET*.
Rowe's *JANE SHORE*.

Appointed an undersearcher of Customs and Secretary to the Island of Jamaica.

1715
Jacobite Rebellion.
Death of Tate.
Rowe made Poet Laureate.
Death of Wycherley.

1716
Addison's *THE DRUMMER*.

1717
David Garrick born.
Cibber's *THE NON-JUROR*.
Gay, Pope, and Arbuthnot's *THREE HOURS AFTER MARRIAGE*.

1718
Death of Rowe.
Centlivre's *A BOLD STROKE FOR A WIFE*.

1719
Death of Addison.
Defoe's *Robinson Crusoe* published.
Young's *BUSIRIS, KING OF EGYPT*.

1720
South Sea Bubble.
Samuel Foote born.

Pope's translation of Homer's *Iliad* dedicated to Congreve.

Steele suspended from the Governorship of Drury Lane (restored 1721).
Little Theatre in the Haymarket opened.
Steele's *The Theatre* (periodical) published.
Hughes' *THE SIEGE OF DAMASCUS*.
Walpole became first Minister.

1722

Steele's *THE CONSCIOUS LOVERS*.

Visited Bath with Henrietta, Duchess of Marlborough, and John Gay.

1723

Death of Susannah Centlivre.
Death of D'Urfey.

Birth on November 23 of Lady Mary Godolphin (afterward Duchess of Leeds), Congreve's daughter by Henrietta, Duchess of Marlborough.

1725

Pope's edition of Shakespeare published.

Made his will on February 26, leaving most of his estate to Henrietta, Duchess of Marlborough.

1726

Death of Jeremy Collier.
Death of Vanbrugh.
Law's *Unlawfulness of Stage Entertainments* published.
Swift's *Gulliver's Travels* published.

Visited by Voltaire.

1727

Death of George I; accession of George II.
Death of Sir Isaac Newton.
Arthur Murphy born.

1728

Pope's *The Dunciad* (first version) published.
Cibber's *THE PROVOKED HUSBAND* (expansion of Vanbrugh's fragment *A JOURNEY TO LONDON*).
Gay's *THE BEGGAR'S OPERA*.

Wrote *Letter to Viscount Cobham*.
In Bath from May through October with Henrietta, Duchess of Marlborough, and Lady Mary Godolphin.

1729

Goodman's Fields Theatre opened.
Death of Steele.
Edmund Burke born.

Died on January 19 in his London lodgings in Surrey Street, off the Strand.
Buried on January 26 in Westminster Abbey.

1730

Cibber made Poet Laureate.
Oliver Goldsmith born.
Thomson's *The Seasons* published.
Fielding's *THE AUTHOR'S FARCE*.
Fielding's *TOM THUMB* (revised as *THE TRAGEDY OF TRAGEDIES*, 1731).

1731

Death of Defoe.
Fielding's *THE GRUB-STREET OPERA*.
Lillo's *THE LONDON MERCHANT*.

1732

Covent Garden Theatre opened.
Death of Gay.
George Colman the elder born.
Fielding's *THE COVENT GARDEN TRAGEDY*.
Fielding's *THE MODERN HUSBAND*.
Charles Johnson's *CAELIA*.

1733

Pope's *An Essay on Man* (Epistles I–III) published (Epistle IV, 1734).

1734

Death of Dennis.
The Prompter began publication (1734–1736).
Theobald's edition of Shakespeare published.
Fielding's *DON QUIXOTE IN ENGLAND*.

1736

Fielding led the "Great Mogul's

Company of Comedians" at the
Little Theatre in the Haymarket
(1736–1737).
Fielding's *PASQUIN*.
Lillo's *FATAL CURIOSITY*.

1737
The State Licensing Act.
Dodsley's *THE KING AND THE
MILLER OF MANSFIELD*.
Fielding's *THE HISTORICAL
REGISTER FOR 1736*.